Keep Your
Gift Plants
Thriving

by Karen Solit with Jim Solit

A Garden Way Publishing Book

STOREY COMMUNICATIONS, INC.
POWNAL, VERMONT 05261

For John and Matthew

Illustrations by Elayne Sears
Design by Andrea Gray

©**Copyright by Storey Communications, Inc.**

The name Garden Way Publishing has been licensed to Storey Communications, Inc. by Garden Way, Inc.

Printed in the United States by Alpine Press
First Printing, August, 1985

Library of Congress Cataloging-in-Publication Data

Solit, Karen, 1950-
  Keep your gift plants thriving.

  Includes index.
    1. House plants. 2. Gifts. I. Solit, Jim.
II. Title. III. Title: Gift plants thriving.
SB419.S565   1985   635.9′65   84-48810
ISBN 0-88266-380-1
ISBN 0-88266-379-8 (pbk.)

CONTENTS

Acknowledgment

I would like to thank the staff of the U.S. Botanic Garden, who shared their horticultural knowledge and talents with me, particularly the late Jimmie L. Crowe.

INTRODUCTION

As a horticulturist for the United States Botanic Garden for five years, I regularly answered telephone calls from men and women requesting advice about plants they had received as gifts. Everyone was pleased with the gift, but anxious about how to maintain a showy blossom for a special event, uncertain about tossing out a plant whose flower had faded and dropped, or sad that a plant gift might be hopelessly lost. In this book I answer all the questions I have ever received on the subject of plant gifts—giving them and receiving them.

A plant is a special gift—because it has life. The attention it requires serves to extend and enhance the original pleasure of the gift. A plant seldom goes out of style, and, if properly cared for, it may provide enjoyment for years—growing larger and lovelier with time. Over the years, I have given and received dozens of beautiful plants. I have never been disappointed upon receipt of a plant gift, and I have never had a dissatisfied recipient. I think the idea of marking an occasion with a renewable living thing transcends the material value and the aesthetic pleasure of the plant itself.

Once you know what to look for, the most difficult thing about buying a plant is choosing among the beautiful varieties available in every season of the year. In the pages that follow, I will tell you how to avoid unhealthy plants, what kind of environment and care different plants require, how to match plants to the people in your life, and how to carry plant gifts over from year to year. A plant purchased in bud or in full bloom is a wonderful gift to receive.

The more ambitious among you may want to increase both your own enjoyment and that of the recipient by raising the plant yourself. You don't need the proverbial green thumb either to keep your own plant gifts alive or to pass the offspring of those plants on to others. Plants, particularly the types discussed in this book, require care. People who care for their plants and meet the proper cultural requirements are successful gardeners; people who think plants care for themselves are not. You cannot count on magic or miracles.

I have experimented and worked with all the plants described in this book. While it would be wonderful to have a greenhouse that imitates the tropical environment enjoyed by many flowering house plants, it certainly isn't necessary. I do just fine without one; my flowering plants thrive in an environment typical of a suburban house or city apartment.

For putting plants outside, however, the part of the country in which you live makes a difference. Throughout the book, I refer to the zones from the United States Department of Agriculture's plant hardiness zone map, in which the country is divided into ten zones. The lower the number, the cooler the zone. For example, most of Vermont is in zone 3, where temperatures dip to -35° F. The southern tip of Florida is zone 10, where temperatures rarely drop below 30° F. The map is included for reference on page 163, at the back of the book.

Most of the materials and products that I use and recommend are available at garden centers, hardware stores, and supermarkets and need no elaboration. However, a few items deserve brief explanations here.

• For propagating plants I often recommend the use of a clear plastic box with a lid, designed for storing shoes or sweaters. This is an item regularly seen in a department store notions department or dime store such as Woolworth's.

• A pebble tray is the most effective means of raising the humidity around a plant. It can be a large saucer or tray filled with pebbles or pea gravel (available at most hardware stores and garden centers). Water is then added, but mustn't be allowed to rise above the top layer of stones since plants sitting in water may suffer root damage. The water must be continually replenished as it evaporates.

• The composition of water-soluble chemical fertilizers varies according to the proportions of the chemicals. When I recommend use of these fertilizers, I also recommend the preferred chemical analysis. The three numbers that I give (and that appear on the product label), such as 15–30–15, always indicate the percentages of nitrogen, phosphorus, and potassium contained in the fertilizer, in that order. There are several products available that are suitable.

With care and knowledge you can have lovely flowering plants in your home throughout the year...and from year to year. You can get the most from plant gifts friends and relatives send you and keep your flower show at its peak for as long as possible. You can propagate your plants and give their progeny as gifts. You also can take your plant gift one step further and tell the recipient how to get year-after-year pleasure from the gift.

The goal of this book is to provide step-by-step information and guidelines that will help everyone—from the first-time giver or receiver to the seasoned plant lover—to derive increased pleasure from giving, receiving, and caring for plants.

PART 1

Plants Offering the Promise of Spring

*See, how gorgeous the world is
Outside the door!*

"Spring Morning"—D.H. Lawrence

As winter's harshness abates and a day of genuine warmth pokes through the otherwise consistent cold, all thoughts turn to spring and its promise of floral bounty. Even anticipating the transition from winter to spring is invigorating. We rarely miss the opportunity to dress for summer early, to get outside and pretend the season actually has changed. I marvel at the originality of each spring as though it were the first one ever.

Spring is the time when nature's warmth, moisture, and light mock the artificially created seasons in greenhouses. Glorious spring provides the chance to suit everyone's fancy with a plant gift, for the variety available at this time is almost endless.

The holidays of spring provide ample opportunity to present gifts. Starting with Saint Patrick's Day, spring includes Easter, National Secretary's Day, May Day, Mother's Day, and Father's Day. The mere fact that spring has arrived is cause for joy, and a gift to celebrate it is always fitting. The wonderful thing about flowering plants exchanged during spring is that each provides a symbol of the season itself, as well as of the holiday commemorated.

In this chapter I discuss eight of the most popular flowering plants available during spring. Each is distinguished by its exotic blossoms. All make terrific gifts and provide lovely symbols of the season—from the large clear colors of the snowball-like hydrangea flowers to the gloxinia with its texture of royal velvet, from the best-selling Easter lily to the azalea, subject of countless festivals honoring its heavenly blossoms.

Unlike most of the plants discussed in this book, a few of the spring flowering beauties should be enjoyed while in bloom, then bravely discarded. The exotic pocketbook plant and the showy cineraria, for example, are treated as annuals without a thought of maintaining them for succeeding seasons. Thankfully, their expendability is more than recompensed by their beauty in bloom.

As always, conditions inside the recipient's home should match the requirements of a gift plant. Yet at this season, when windows are thrown open and the dry indoor heat of winter is replaced by the natural elements, finding a suitable match is not in the least difficult. Proper placement of a plant may be on the porch or patio instead of on the coffee table.

AZALEA

Special Spring Gift

Scientific Name: *Rhododendron*
   species and hybrids
Origin: Worldwide

In parts of America where conditions encourage the successful cultivation of azaleas outdoors, everyone knows and loves them. They fill the gardens and parks in and around Washington, making early spring in the Capitol City a glorious sight and a favorite season for tourists and residents alike. Azaleas are second in popularity only to Washington's world-famous cherry blossoms.

The Southeast is not the only part of the country boasting excellent conditions for growing azaleas. The Pacific Northwest, especially around Seattle, is also an ideal spot for their cultivation. The western azaleas are sometimes a shock to easterners, who foolishly believe they have a patent on these beauties. There are, however, parts of the United States where azaleas do not grow well for one reason or another; either summers are too hot, winters are too cold, or soil conditions are inappropriate. Those living outside azalea-growing territory will have to take my word for it: Where they grow outside, azaleas mean spring, so they are the perfect gift with which to commemorate the season.

Description

Though most azaleas are deciduous and can reach heights of up to 15 feet, the azaleas grown for holiday gift giving are evergreen shrubs, generally up to 2 feet high. They have small oval-oblong leaves and funnel-shaped flowers produced in clusters at the stem tips. There is a wide color range including white and shades of pink, salmon, crimson, magenta, and orange, as well as several bicolored forms. Some have single five-petaled flowers; others bear double multi-petaled blossoms. Most azaleas bloom naturally in early spring but can be forced for earlier flowering or held back to bloom at a later date. Azaleas are a subgroup of the genus *Rhododendron*, which explains why many varieties of the two plants resemble each other.

Azaleas are classified into groups, usually based on common ancestry. The type most often grown in greenhouses as a gift plant is nicknamed Indian azalea after one of the species from which it supposedly originated, *Rhododendron indicum*. Indian azaleas are also referred to as large-flowered azaleas since their blossoms are up to 3 inches across. They are not hardy outdoors except in the very warmest parts of the country, which explains their third nickname, greenhouse azalea.

5

Kurume azaleas (*Rhododendron* hybrids) are also grown in containers as gifts, though they are best known as garden shrubs in zones 6 to 9. Kurumes are hardier than the Indians. They bear smaller flowers, up to 1½ inches across; their leaves are smaller; and they have a thicker growth habit.

Availability

Since it is possible for commercial growers to have azaleas in flower year-round, a search of major garden centers and florist shops should uncover a source at any season. Plants are most plentiful, however, around Christmas—when red-flowered varieties dominate—Valentine's Day, Mother's Day, and, of course, Easter.

Selection

When buying a plant, you want to select a healthy, vigorous specimen with a bushy habit, rich, green unmarred foliage, and a generous supply of yet-to-open flower buds. You should not have much trouble finding a worthy specimen, but you must be on the lookout for a number of problems to which azaleas are prone. This is a plant you will surely want the recipient to keep for years, and special care should be taken in making a choice. I have listed the major maladies to beware of.

• The wilt organisms that affect azaleas cause young leaves to yellow and droop. If the soil is moist and leaves have wilted, suspect a problem and continue your search.

• Flower spot or azalea petal blight produces pale, circular, pinhead-sized spots on the undersides of infected flower petals. Eventually the spots enlarge and grow together, creating white blotches on colored flowers and brown blotches on white blossoms. Ultimately the entire flower collapses.

• A number of fungi cause discolored, irregularly shaped leaf spots on azaleas. In severe cases leaves will drop.

• Leaf yellowing often occurs when plants are grown in overly alkaline soil, which ties up available iron and causes discoloration.

• Spider mites, aphids, whiteflies, mealybugs, and scale insects are described in Part 5.

Cultural Requirements

The most common mistake made with newly acquired azaleas is providing an inadequate amount of water. Most plants found in the shops are fairly pot-bound since they flower most heavily in undersized containers. As a result, the soil tends to dry rapidly between waterings. If not kept properly moistened, plants will droop miserably and shed leaves at a horrifying rate. Other azalea care is relatively straightforward.

LIGHT: Since azaleas require 4 hours of very bright sunlight each day, placing the plant close to a window is essential. A northern exposure that receives indirect light will do nicely. A southern or eastern exposure where the sun's strong afternoon rays are filtered through sheer curtains or partially closed shutters also fills the bill.

TEMPERATURE: Night temperatures of 45–55° F. and day temperatures of 68° F. or less are perfect to prolong flower freshness and keep your plant in top form.

MOISTURE: Check daily to see if the top layer of soil in the container feels dry to the touch. If so, soak thoroughly by pouring water into the soil until it runs through the drainage holes in the bottom of the pot. Wait about 15 minutes and *again* water thoroughly. Discard any excess moisture that accumulates in the drip plate beneath the pot about a half-hour after the double soaking.

FERTILIZER: There is no need to fertilize an azalea while it is in bloom.

PLACEMENT IN THE HOME: Since this plant requires low night temperatures, it will probably have to be set in a cool entranceway or enclosed porch during the evening. However, when entertaining, feel free to move it to where it can be seen. No harm will be done as long as it is returned within a day or so to an area where conditions are appropriate.

After Flowers Fade

Each year, container-grown Indian azaleas are featured as part of the U.S. Botanic Garden's annual Spring Flower Show. Many are ages old and as large as any potted specimens I have seen. They are stupendous, literally coated with flowers, and almost steal the show. These plants are a testament to the fact that azaleas can be carried over from year to year, becoming larger and more floriferous with time.

Azaleas do, however, require cool growing conditions, a problem for gardenless gardeners to provide. Perhaps apartment dwellers would be best off giving their azaleas to a house owner once the flowers have faded. This way you can have the dual pleasures of receiving an azalea in bloom and giving one that promises to bloom the following year.

LIGHT, TEMPERATURE, MOISTURE, AND FERTILIZER: After the azalea has bloomed, provide 4 hours of direct sunlight daily. Maintain temperatures of 45–55° F. at night and 68° F. or lower by day. Water as described when the top layer of soil begins to feel dry.

Begin fertilizing with an acid-type fertilizer recommended for use on azaleas every 2 weeks from the time the flowers fade until late summer when new flower buds form. Withhold fertilizer after that point. If the leaves on your azalea turn yellow between the veins, apply a chelated iron product (available at garden centers) according to package directions.

POTTING AND SOIL: After plants bloom, pinch off the faded blossoms and repot into a new container that is 1 inch larger in diameter than the old pot. Be sure not to overpot; azaleas flower best in tight containers. A mixture of 2 parts peat moss, 1 part packaged potting soil, and 1 part builder's sand or perlite is suitable.

PLANTING AZALEAS PERMANENTLY OUTDOORS: In warmer parts of the country, zones 6 to 9, kurume azaleas can be planted in the garden during spring, after they have finished blooming. In the deep South, zones 8 to 10, Indian azaleas can also be given a permanent spot outdoors. Obviously, knowing which type of azalea you have is essential. If in doubt, take your azalea to a garden center or plant shop and ask to have it identified.

Azaleas require acid soil; a pH of approximately 5.5 is perfect. If in doubt about the acidity of your soil, use litmus paper, obtainable in most hardware stores or garden centers, to test it; or have your soil checked by the Cooperative Extension Service in your town. This organization is usually listed in the telephone book under "County Government."

Azaleas thrive in partial sun, although they also perform well in rather deeply shaded spots. Azaleas make wonderful foundation plants (plants grown around the foundation of a building, set against a house or other structure). They are also perfect in woodland gardens and along lightly shaded paths. The effect of mixed color groupings can be spectacular. If you live in azalea-growing territory, you should have no trouble identifying a perfect setting for your plant.

PLACING THE AZALEA TEMPORARILY OUTDOORS: In cooler parts of the country where evergreen azaleas will not survive winter temperatures, they should be placed temporarily outdoors during warm weather. After the danger of frost has passed, plunge the pot up to its rim in a well-drained spot that receives morning sunlight and dappled shade during the afternoon. Remember to fertilize every 2 weeks until buds form at the end of summer. Water plants during dry spells. Shrubs in containers plunged into the earth dry more quickly than those in open soil, since the roots have no place to go in search of moisture. Therefore, it will be necessary to check the soil often during hot dry periods.

BRINGING PLANTS BACK INSIDE IN AUTUMN: Unless you live in zone 8, 9, or 10, the Indian azaleas must be overwintered indoors, because they will not survive the temperatures in cooler parts of the country. So before the danger of autumn frost, bring those azaleas that would not survive the winter in your area back inside. Place them in a cool sunny spot where temperatures are in the 45–55° F. range. Warmer temperatures are one of the major reasons people get a skimpy supply of flowers. Once the flower buds are well formed and show color, plants can be moved into a warmer room during the day. Once in bloom, provide azaleas with the same care as described under "Cultural Requirements," page 6.

PRUNING: To assure a bushy, well-branched habit, azaleas should be shaped and pruned annually, immediately after they finish blooming. If this job is delayed, you may unwittingly cut off next year's flower buds. The pinching off of spent blossoms and the annual pruning should be performed concurrently.

There is another pruning chore often recommended for growing professional-quality azaleas. It is the removal of the tiny green shoots that develop around and often cover new flower buds. Some professionals believe that this growth should be removed as soon as it appears because it diverts nutrients from the buds and may cause them to dry before opening, and because it hides the flowers. A second flush of growth should appear after the plants flower, and this growth should be left since it will carry the following year's blossoms.

An Important Tip: Indoors, developing azalea buds should be misted with tepid water to keep the calyx soft, so that the buds can emerge easily and without deformity. (The calyx consists of sepals or leaf-like structures that initially enclose the flower buds and eventually underlie them.)

Propagation

Azaleas are propagated from tip cuttings taken in late summer. Cuttings can be rooted in a clear plastic box (see page 87) filled with equal parts of evenly moistened peat moss and perlite. Pot newly rooted cuttings individually in 3-inch pots filled with the same mix. Pinch them back right after planting and several times during the growing season to promote branching. Follow the same pattern for care as you would for the mother plant, including placement outdoors during mild weather.

GLOXINIA

The African Violet's Most Glamorous Relative

Scientific Name: *Sinningia speciosa*
Origin: Brazil

With its brilliant, long-lasting flowers and velvety texture, the gloxinia is indeed a relative of the African violet. Yet the gloxinia's special cultural needs and the ample space a full-grown specimen requires often make it a bit less endearing than its more famous cousin. In addition, while the African violet rewards its owner with several sets of blossoms each year in exchange for minimal care, the gloxinia bears a single flush of flowers after trying the patience—and to some extent the horticultural talents—of its owner. However, once you have seen a gloxinia in full bloom, any extra bother is sure to seem worthwhile. A gloxinia is the perfect gift choice for African-violet connoisseurs. The plants have similar requirements and make perfect display companions.

Gloxinias are the source of some botanical confusion. The gloxinias discussed here are hybrids of the plant *Sinningia speciosa*. There are also tiny gloxinias belonging to the same genus (*Sinningia*), some less than 3 inches across, which most folks call sinningias. Generally, when you hear the word "sinningia," the miniature gloxinias are the subject, whereas the term "gloxinia" should conjure an image of the showier members of this group, also called florists' gloxinias. To add to the confusion, there is another group of plants with the genus name *Gloxinia*. Fortunately, they are not commonly cultivated and are rarely found in the shops.

Description

The beautiful flowers of gloxinias, 3 inches or more across, are either bell-shaped or slipper-shaped and are held on stiff stalks above the foliage. Colors include rich purple, deep red, white, lavender, and pink. The texture is as plush as a king's velvet robe. Blossoms are often marked with a contrasting hue, in the form of either bands or speckles. There are single-flowered varieties as well as multi-petaled double forms.

In addition to stupendous flowers, gloxinias produce velvety oval leaves, up to 8 inches across. Like African violets, a single plant may bear either a symmetrical rosette of foliage or several rosettes arranged in a helter-skelter pattern, depending on variety and growing techniques.

Gloxinias grow from a tuber, a modified underground stem that looks like a bulb. Like most other tuberous plants, they require a rest between flowerings. Many people become uneasy at the thought of raising plants from tubers, knowing they require a dormant period. To shy away from gloxinias for this reason is to cheat yourself out of growing one of the indoor garden's most spectacular subjects. In fact, forcing a gloxinia to rest is not particularly difficult, nor is urging it to begin growing again. It is simply a matter of knowing what to do when. Moreover, as far as tuberous rooted plants are concerned, the gloxinia is relatively easy to handle.

Availability

Though in nature they bloom in late summer, flowering gloxinia plants are most plentiful in the shops during late winter and early spring, making them popular for Easter and early spring giving. As with so many other plants, growers can produce them for other seasons by using artificial lights and controlling greenhouse temperatures. Unfortunately, spring-blooming gloxinias that have been forced by growers tend to perform poorly in comparison to specimens that are home-grown from tubers planted for late summer bloom. If you have a choice, grow gloxinias from scratch, as described on page 14. It is quite easy, even for a novice.

Selection

To get your money's worth out of a full-grown blooming plant, choose one with healthy leaves and plenty of yet-to-open flower buds. Look for a compact habit. Plants that are stretched and leggy were probably grown in poor light or overcrowded conditions. Check closely for spider mites on leaf undersides and examine leaf axils for the presence of mealy bugs. Make sure there are no soft or rotten spots at the base of the plant where the stem meets the soil line. Select a plant that bears the full complement of leaves; gloxinia foliage is brittle, and leaves are easily broken in shipment.

Cultural Requirements

Following are some simple instructions for the care of a gloxinia plant in bloom. Due to improper watering or too little light, most people do not get the full show from their plants. Special attention should be paid to those requirements.

LIGHT: Gloxinias require at least 4 hours of very bright indirect natural light, or 12 to 14 hours of artificial fluorescent light, daily. Insufficient light will cause leaves to stretch upward. Too much natural light in summer may cause scorching, though this is rarely a problem in other seasons.

Plants grown on a windowsill should be given a quarter turn every week to prevent them from leaning toward the light and losing their natural symmetry.

I think the best gloxinias are grown under fluorescent lights, just as African violets and many other members of the gesneriad family are. Plants should be placed within 6 inches of a standard 4-foot, two-tube fluorescent fixture equipped with one cool and one warm white 40-watt tube. Fluorescent light fixtures are available from variety stores.

TEMPERATURE: Most growers recommend night temperatures of 65–70° F. and day temperatures of 75° F. I grow my gloxinias in a cool cellar where night winter temperatures go down to 55° F. My gloxinias fare beautifully; I think they are sturdier and more compact than most others I see. Naturally, plants must be slowly acclimated to such low temperatures.

MOISTURE: Irrigate when the top layer of soil in the container feels dry to the touch. Then water thoroughly until water runs through the drainage holes in the bottom of the pot. To prevent foliage discoloration and spotting, avoid splashing water on the leaves.

Since gloxinias grow best where relative humidity is in the 50–60 percent range, set pots on a pebble tray—a watertight tray filled with well-moistened pea gravel. The water will evaporate and humidify the air surrounding the plant.

FERTILIZER: Gloxinias do not require fertilizer while they are in bloom.

PLACEMENT IN THE HOME: Feel free to move your gloxinia out from under the lights or off the windowsill when you entertain. This plant looks especially beautiful when placed where it can be viewed from above, such as on a coffee table. Also, gloxinias are sensational when displayed with African violets. After an evening or afternoon in the compliment corner, return the plant to its growing area.

After Flowers Fade

Caring for a gloxinia after the flowers have faded entails allowing the plant to take a brief rest, forcing it to begin growing again, and, finally, providing the care that will ultimately result in another flush of gorgeous blossoms. As always, you have the choice of tossing the plant out and starting over again with a new tuber or specimen. But I would at least *try* to carry the gloxinia over. You may be pleasantly surprised.

FORCING A REST: Once flowers have faded and there are no unopened buds tucked under the foliage, cut off all top growth as close to the tuber as possible—even if the leaves are still green. You may find tiny new shoots just emerging from the tuber. If so, leave them alone—they are the beginning of a new flush of growth. Gesneriad specialists have taught us that you do not need to allow the foliage to yellow and wither gradually before cutting it off, as with other bulbous plants, in order for the tuber to "ripen" and get ready to produce new growth.

REPOTTING AND SOIL MIXTURE: After the top growth has been removed, carefully repot the leafless tuber in an azalea pan, a clay container available from garden centers which is wider and shorter than a standard pot. Do not worry if the original pot was not an azalea pan. The new container should be only ½ inch larger in diameter than the old one. Place clay shards over the drainage holes in the bottom of the pot to prevent it from clogging with soil.

When repotting, try not to disturb the roots, which are still functioning. Repot at a depth that will leave the top of the tuber even with the soil surface. It should not be buried underground. Surface planting will help prevent rot—a common problem with all bulbous and tuberous plants. A potting mix of 2 parts peat moss, 1 part packaged potting soil, and 1 part perlite is ideal. Gloxinia tubers sprout in about 8 weeks, though this varies considerably depending on variety and environmental conditions.

LIGHT, TEMPERATURE, MOISTURE, AND FERTILIZER: Provide the newly potted tuber with the same amount of light you would a full-grown specimen—either 4 hours of very bright indirect light or 12 to 14 hours of artificial light each day. This way the plant will be subjected to the appropriate light level as soon as growth begins, and the young shoots will not become stretched and leggy, as they might if new growth were made in low light levels.

Water the newly scalped tuber only when the top *half* of soil in the pan feels totally dry. Then irrigate thoroughly, until water runs through the drainage holes in the bottom of the pot. Once new growth begins, set plants on a pebble tray to increase humidity. Start watering when the top layer of soil in the pot feels dry. Provide the exact same temperatures as recommended under "Cultural Requirements," page 11.

Do not begin fertilizing until new growth is produced. Then fertilize every 2 weeks with a water-soluble chemical product recommended for use on house plants, at one-half the strength suggested on the label. Once the leaves have grown above the pot's rim, fertilize every 2 weeks at the full strength recommended.

Soon you will have a magnificent specimen full of flowers, and you can follow the same instructions for its care as provided under "Cultural Requirements," page 11. I would not carry a gloxinia over for more than 3 years, as they become less productive after that.

PRUNING: Often, more than one shoot grows from a single gloxinia tuber. All but the strongest one should be cut off as close to the tuber as possible while they are still very small. Gloxinia flowers, like those of the African violet, look best when growing out from the center of a single symmetrical plant.

Growing Gloxinias from Tubers

The best gloxinias are started from scratch. They are grown slowly from tubers under average home conditions, not quickly forced in a warm, humid greenhouse. Aside from the satisfaction of raising glorious flowering beauties from knotty looking tubers, home-grown plants tend to be sturdier and bloom over a longer time period.

Tubers are usually available in the shops during spring. Of course, they can be ordered at any season from nurseries specializing in gesneriads; several are listed in the appendix. When buying tubers, select large, firm specimens. If you find one with a tiny shoot already sprouted, all the better—you have got a head start. If you shop by mail, you will simply have to trust your source.

Plants begin growing 1 to 8 weeks after the tuber is planted. Ideally, tubers are started in late winter or early spring and bloom around July or August. Those started in the autumn will bloom in about 5 months.

- Place clay shards over the drainage holes in the bottom of a 4–6-inch azalea pan. The shards will help prevent the hole from becoming clogged with soil and will stop the soil from running out.
- Fill the pot with the mix recommended on page 13. Set the tuber on the soil surface—dead center—knotty-side up, and gently twist it in so that the tuber surface is level with the soil surface.
- Tap the pot against a hard surface several times to firm the soil around the tuber.
- Soak the soil thoroughly with tepid water.
- Begin providing the same care as outlined under "Light, Temperature, Moisture, and Fertilizer" on page 13.

Propagation by Cuttings

Gloxinias are also propagated by leaf cuttings, which include the blade plus about 1 inch of leaf stalk. A healthy, fresh, full-grown leaf taken from a plant before it is in bud or bloom is best. Gloxinia leaves can be rooted like those of the African violet, as described on page 104. During the rooting process keep the leaves warm, around 70° F.

Once the leaf has rooted, plant it in a 2½–3-inch pot filled with the mix described on page 13. Water the cutting as you would the mother plant, when the top soil layer feels dry, and place it in bright indirect sunlight or under a fluorescent fixture. Approximately 6 weeks after potting, new leaves will appear at the base of the mother leaf.

Once the leaves have grown above the pot's rim, transplant into a 4-inch azalea pan. Soon after, pinch off all but the strongest shoot, since more than one new plant is likely to grow around the base of the newly rooted leaf. Then begin the exact same care as described under "Light, Temperature, Moisture, and Fertilizer" on page 13.

Repot the young gloxinia as needed—when roots grow through the drainage holes in the bottom of the pot, when water runs through the soil unusually fast between waterings, or when the soil dries quickly between irrigations. As with other plants, repot into a container only 1 inch larger in diameter than the old one. Tubers will form underground on plants started from leaf cuttings.

HYDRANGEA

A Spectacular Spring Bloomer

Scientific Name: *Hydrangea macrophylla*
Origin: Japan

Sometimes a plant's appeal is as subject to the whims of a fickle public as hem lines or hair styles, and for a while the once popular potted hydrangeas seemed to have gone the way of miniskirts and pompadours. Although changing taste accounts for its share of this trend, the greater reason is that the potted hydrangeas available until recently were often of poor quality and simply did not make good purchases. Within the past several years, however, improved specimens and better hybrids have become available as potted plants, and the public has begun to appreciate the lavish flowers, luscious colors, and excellent indoor-keeping qualities of hydrangeas. Their enormous snowball-like blossoms are now a familiar sight in florist shops and garden centers during spring and early summer. The fabulous blooms last and last, making the plant an excellent gift.

Description

The bigleaf or house hydrangea (*Hydrangea macrophylla*) is well known as a potted holiday plant, but better known and more widely grown as a shrub. The hydrangea's sometimes flashy appearance belies the fact that they are familiar to gardens of the Orient where delicacy, order, and beauty in the landscape arts are the result of centuries-old tradition.

Hydrangeas are also widely grown in American gardens, particularly in the South and along coastal areas. In fact, the bigleaf hydrangea is always included on the rather limited list of plants suitable for seashore planting—a trying environment that it tolerates remarkably well. Since this plant's northernmost limit is zone 5, an area that reaches into southern Massachusetts, it is less frequently cultivated in colder climes. However, plants are grown successfully as far north as Cape Cod when placed in protected areas.

Planted in the open soil, the bigleaf hydrangea generally reaches a height of 4–6 feet. Potted flowering specimens are usually in the 18–24-inch range. Blossoms are produced at the tips of upright woody stems. The oval leaves, 2–6 inches long, are smooth and a shiny rich green.

Bigleaf hydrangea flowers are extravagant, to say the least. The snowball types, those that produce the familiar rounded floral clusters, 5–10 inches in diameter, are the most popular of the bigleaf clan. Their colors include white, shades of pink, red, blue, and mauve, and combinations of these hues, depending on which of the approximately fifty varieties is being grown. The floral clusters are composed of male and female flowers. The male or "ray" flowers (bearing pollen but incapable of producing seeds) bear showy colored sepals that cover the floral head. These sepals resemble and are frequently mistaken for petals. Actually, the petals are quite inconspicuous. The less dramatic female flowers (seed producing) are hidden in the floral cluster.

Another form of bigleaf hydrangea is the lace-cap. It produces a more flattened bloom, which to me is more pleasing and delicate. The female flowers form the center of the lace-cap flower cluster, and the more ornate males are produced in an outer ring. This type is well worth shopping around for.

The flower color of bigleaf hydrangeas depends not only on the variety grown, but also on the level of acidity in the soil, a factor known as soil pH. This makes them something of a horticultural oddity. The aluminum content of the soil is responsible for flower color. Aluminum is present in all soils, but it cannot be taken up by the plant if the soil is too alkaline. For the most part, hydrangea flowers are blue if the soil is acid, making aluminum available, and pink if the soil is alkaline, a condition which ties up the aluminum. The white-flowered types are an exception; they remain white regardless of soil conditions.

Growers can control color with various fertilizer treatments during the production period. For example, if pink flowers are desired, they might add limestone or hydrated lime to raise the soil pH to around 6 or 6.5—which is fairly alkaline. For blue flowers, iron or aluminum sulfate can be dissolved in the irrigation water to bring the pH down to about 5.0.

The bigleaf is one of about forty-five hydrangea species, several of which are important landscape plants. Three other widely planted species are the climbing hydrangea (*Hydrangea anomala petiolaris*), an exquisite clinging woody vine; the peegee hydrangea (*Hydrangea paniculata* Grandiflora), with long-lasting, cream-colored, pyramidal blossoms up to 18 inches long, on tree-shaped plants up to 25 feet high; and the oakleaf hydrangea (*Hydrangea quercifolia*), named for the shape of its leaves, which, like its namesake, have wonderful fall color.

Availability

Potted flowering hydrangeas are most abundant during spring. As a consequence, they are closely associated with Easter and Mother's Day gift giving. Flowering plants could be produced at other seasons, but they would require a long period of controlled greenhouse temperatures, an increasingly costly proposition that would surely be passed on to consumers in the form of higher-priced plants. In contrast, the growing schedule for spring and early summer flowering hydrangeas relies on natural weather conditions for most of the production period, keeping retail costs down.

Selection

When shopping for a hydrangea, look for healthy, rich green foliage and fresh, clear-colored blossoms. Also keep an eye out for the following problems:

• A yellowing of the leaves between the veins may be caused by an iron deficiency, poor root growth, an inadequate nitrogen supply, or overly alkaline soil.

• The absence of lower leaves is often the result of overcrowding, pest damage, or a moisture imbalance.

• A cottony fungus growth on the leaves, called "powdery mildew," is a common hydrangea malady, discussed in detail on page 157. It often is caused by a combination of cool nights and poor air circulation around plants during the growing period.

• Spider mites, aphids, and cyclamen mites are described in Part 5.

Cultural Requirements

You have only to meet a few simple requirements to keep the flowers on your newly acquired hydrangea fresh for several weeks. Even the eventual decline of the blooms is accompanied by an appealing softening of their color, a phenomenon which prolongs the period of enjoyment. The most common potted-hydrangea blunder is underwatering, a practice which can result in a speedy, irrevocable, and untimely decline.

LIGHT: Provide bright indirect light such as that found in front of an unobstructed northern window. Too much light may cause flowers to droop.

TEMPERATURE: Night temperatures of 55–60° F. and day temperatures of 68–72° F. are ideal for prolonging flower freshness.

MOISTURE: Hydrangeas require an abundance of water, and you will find that the top layer of soil in the container dries unusually fast between waterings. It is important to feel the soil daily. When the top layer is dry, water thoroughly, until water runs through the drainage holes in the bottom of the container.

FERTILIZER: Fertilizer is not required during the blooming period.

PLACEMENT IN THE HOME: Since the hydrangea is such a lavish subject, it generally looks best displayed alone. In fact, I really cannot think of any plant it would complement and not overshadow—except, of course, another hydrangea.

After Flowers Fade

Regardless of where you live, after the hydrangea flowers have faded, the plant should be cut back to about 1 inch above the old growth. You can distinguish between old and new growth because the young wood is green and the old wood is brown. Such severe pruning may seem drastic, but it is essential to the production of new growth on which flowers will form.

Where the climate permits, in parts of zone 5 and southward, hydrangeas can be planted permanently in the garden; subsequent blooms inside the home will not nearly match the possibilities outside. In northern parts of zone 5 and northward, this plant cannot tolerate the low winter temperatures and must be brought back indoors after the first autumn frost.

THE HYDRANGEA OUTDOORS: Fortunately, this plant is not finicky, and in exchange for a few simple requirements it provides a yearly bounty of blossoms which can be left on the plant to highlight your summer garden or cut for a rich-looking indoor display. A single bloom can fill a large vase.

SITE SELECTION AND SOIL: Select a well-drained site for planting. If the soil has a high clay content (easily detected by its red color and sticky feel), dig in some organic matter such as compost or peat moss to improve the texture. Choose a spot that will allow the shrub to reach its potential size. Hydrangeas grow quickly to 6 feet in height *and* width—12 feet if undamaged by low winter temperatures and left unpruned. If you live as far north as zone 5, try and choose a protected spot, such as near the house or behind a windbreak, that still meets the plant's light requirements.

LIGHT: The most floriferous specimens I have seen are grown in full sun, though hydrangeas tolerate and also flower well in light shade.

MOISTURE: The hydrangea should be deeply watered during dry periods, especially the first year after planting, when its roots are not well established.

FERTILIZER: If you have planted your hydrangea where the soil is high in nutrients, you will probably not need to fertilize. Otherwise, you should apply a dry slow-release fertilizer in early spring when growth begins, or supply a liquid feed throughout the growing season. Be sure to follow the package directions carefully, regardless of which product you choose.

PRUNING: Shrubs planted outdoors should be pruned in very early spring, before new growth begins. Cut back shoots that flowered the previous summer to within two pairs of buds from ground level. (The spent blossoms will probably have remained throughout winter, so you will have no trouble determining which branches have bloomed.) Also, cut out weak stems and any frost-damaged wood. Neglected plants soon become stubby and unattractive. Old plants in need of rejuvenation can be sheared to ground level in early spring, resulting in dramatically improved specimens within a few years.

SETTING THE HYDRANGEA OUT: In colder parts of zone 5 and northward, after the pruning that follows the indoor-blooming period, repot the hydrangea in a container about 2 inches larger than the original one. Equal parts of packaged potting soil, peat moss, and perlite make a suitable growing medium.

Place the newly potted plant in a sunny part of the garden after danger of frost has passed. To avoid wind damage, you can sink the pot up to its rim in the soil. Remember, hydrangeas require frequent irrigation, especially when temperatures are high, so check the potting soil often.

After the first hard autumn frost, bring the plant into a cold but frost-free cellar or garage and leave it there. Water the hydrangea often enough to keep the soil moist, until around the first week of February. It is important that the existing stems do not die during this period, because they are bearing next summer's flower buds. Hydrangeas bloom on old wood, not new growth.

After the first week in February, bring the plant into a sunny room that is about 50° F. at night for about 3 weeks. Then move it to a spot where temperatures are in the 65–70° F. range, and set it on a sunny windowsill. Continue to water freely when the top layer of soil feels dry to the touch. Once the plant is in bloom, provide the same care as described under "Cultural Requirements," page 18.

Propagation

Hydrangeas are easily propagated by cuttings taken from the new growth that is produced after plants have been pruned.

• Take a 4–5-inch cutting just above a node, the point where a leaf joins the stem.

• Remove the bottom pair of leaves from the cutting and dip the base of the cut stem in a rooting powder, a plant-growth hormone available in most garden centers.

- Fill a 3-inch plastic pot with equal parts of peat moss and perlite.
- Moisten the mix thoroughly and insert the cutting.
- Cover the newly inserted cutting with clear plastic wrap, making sure the plastic is held above the cutting. Bamboo stakes or wire hoops fashioned from coat hangers can be used for this purpose. Use a rubberband to secure the plastic wrap to the sides of the pot.
- Set the pot in a spot that receives indirect light.
- If the cutting has been well watered and the plastic is sealed tight around the pot, it will probably need no further attention until rooting has occurred. This should take 3 to 4 weeks.
- Once rooted, plant the cutting in a 3-inch pot containing equal parts of packaged potting soil, peat moss, and perlite.
- After potting, keep it out of direct light for about a week and set it on a pebble tray to keep the humidity high and prevent wilting.
- Place the cutting on a sunny windowsill.
- Begin watering when the top soil layer feels dry, and fertilize monthly with a water-soluble chemical fertilizer high in phosphorus.
- Once the cutting has outgrown its container, repot into a 5-inch pot, using the mix just described. Hydrangeas have outgrown their containers when you see roots growing through the drainage holes in the bottom of the pot, when the soil dries unusually fast between waterings, or when water runs quickly through the soil after irrigation.
- Once the young plant is well established in its new container and the danger of frost has passed, put the potted plant outdoors in the earth, exactly as described under "Setting the Hydrangea Out," page 20.

EASTER LILY

Holiday Symbol

Scientific Name: *Lilium longiflorum*
Origin: Orient

Easter lilies are to Easter what poinsettias are to Christmas—living symbols of the holiday. As the red bracts and green foliage of a poinsettia represent the Christmas color scheme, the snow-white flowers of an Easter lily commemorate the purity of Easter and herald the coming of spring. And, like their Yuletide counterparts, they are raised by the millions every year by commercial growers who carefully coax them into bloom for Easter gift giving.

Each year I admire the bounty of picture-perfect Easter lilies in plant shops and supermarkets, noting their remarkable uniformity. The rows of Easter lilies look as if they just rolled off nature's assembly line. Plant professionals not only produce marvelous plants, they also meet the annual challenge of bringing the rather finicky Easter lily into bloom right on time, a particularly trying feat when you consider that Easter arrives on a different date each year. This is truly a testament to the extraordinary talents of contemporary growers.

Description

The sweetly scented, funnel-shaped white flowers of the Easter lily are 6–8 inches long and 4–5 inches wide. The flowers are produced atop leafy stems, 1–3 feet high. At one time, the variety named Croft, which reaches a height of over 2 feet, was highly favored, but in recent years it has taken a back seat to such improved forms as Ace, which is a bit more compact but just as floriferous, and Nellie White, a strong grower also of a slightly smaller stature.

The pure white petals of the Easter lily contrast strikingly with the bright yellow pollen grains at the tips of the anthers, the threadlike structures produced from inside the blossoms. The pollen-bearing anthers are one of the most interesting and ornamental features of Easter lily flowers, indeed of all lilies. Regrettably, growers and florists often pinch off the pollen sacs in order to preserve a "lily-white" flower, unstained by yellow pollen grains, and to prolong the life of the flower. This effort seems unnecessarily compulsive to me. As far as I can determine, cool temperatures and appropriate light levels keep the flowers fresh for plenty of time. The advantages of removing the pollen sacs do not warrant destroying the natural character and beauty of the flowers.

Easter lilies are among hundreds of lily species, a group prized for their unsurpassable beauty, stately habit, and gorgeously colored delicate blossoms. All lilies grow from a bulb composed of fleshy scales, not from a solid structure like the tulip bulb. Most lilies flower in summer (including the Easter lily, which is artificially forced for spring bloom). All lilies are perennial. They produce foliage in spring, flower in summer, and die back to the ground during winter, a cycle repeated annually.

Availability

Easter lilies are available almost exclusively from a few weeks before Easter through the big day. Budded and blooming plants are sold everywhere from supermarkets to corner florist shops. You should not have any trouble tracking down an absolutely perfect specimen.

Selection

Most Easter lilies found in the marketplace are of wonderfully high quality, but there are a few points you should keep in mind when making a selection in order to get the best buy.

• To get the longest possible show from an Easter lily, select a plant with one or two lower flowers opened and the upper buds just beginning to show the white color of the blossoms.

• If you have an opinion one way or the other about removal of the pollen sacs, check this feature out. I prefer to buy a plant on which they have been left intact. Of course, the flowers that open in your home will have their pollen sacs.

• Avoid plants that have lost lower leaves. This is usually caused by a lack of nitrogen, poor soil aeration, a lack of water, or overcrowding—a condition that results in light deficiency.

• Aphids are the chief Easter-lily pest; check closely for infestation.

• Avoid buying a plant with leaf-tip burn, a common problem caused by improper soil pH or a nutrient imbalance.

• Select a plant with plenty of flower buds. A specimen that has produced less than the plant's potential number may have been grown from a puny bulb, a bulb stored too long before potting, or one allowed to dry in storage. Check other plants in the shops for comparison, so you will know to avoid a sparsely budded specimen.

• Do not buy a plant that shows signs of blight. This common disorder causes discolored circular or oval spots on leaves and flowers.

Cultural Requirements

There is nothing complicated about caring for a newly acquired Easter lily. Nevertheless, it is important to remember that, as with other bulbous plants, too much moisture can cause the speedy and untimely decline of this beauty.

LIGHT: An Easter lily in bloom should be provided with bright indirect light such as that found in front of a northern window. A sunnier exposure where the bright afternoon sun is filtered through sheer curtains, partially closed Venetian blinds, or shrubs growing outside the window is also suitable.

TEMPERATURE: Night temperatures of 45–60° F. and day temperatures of 68° F. or lower are ideal for prolonging flower freshness.

MOISTURE: Water thoroughly only when the top layer of soil feels very dry to the touch, not before. Too much water may cause the bulb to rot.

FERTILIZER: There is no need to fertilize an Easter lily while it is in bloom.

PLACEMENT IN THE HOME: Since the Easter lily does best with low night temperatures, you may need to place it on an unheated porch or in a cool entranceway during the night. It can be moved to the living area during the day—just remember to provide appropriate light levels.

Since this plant is relatively tall, it should be placed where it can be viewed from a distance. A coffee table set in the center of a small room may not be the spot where this plant will be displayed to its best advantage; a dining room buffet set against a wall is perfect.

After Flowers Fade

Caring for an Easter lily after it has flowered entails the same basic principles as maintaining other bulbous plants, including the amaryllis and the hardy bulbs discussed in Part 2. The flowers are pinched off after they fade, but the flower stalk and foliage are left intact to produce the nutrients for next year's blossoms. If the green growth is removed, the bulb may come up "blind" the following year—without any flowers at all.

LIGHT, TEMPERATURE, MOISTURE, AND FERTILIZER: After the plant has bloomed, place it on a windowsill that receives a few hours of direct sunlight daily. Normal indoor temperatures are just fine. Water exactly as you have been. After the flowers have been removed, fertilize every 2 weeks with a water-soluble chemical fertilizer recommended for use on flowering house plants. Apply the product at one-half the strength suggested on the label.

PLANTING OUTDOORS: It is very difficult to carry over an Easter lily from one year to the next indoors, unless you have a greenhouse and some type of cool storage area. Assuming you are like me and do not, the best way to insure the survival of your lily is to plant it outdoors in the garden. In fact, if you have a yard, there is absolutely no reason to discard the Easter lily after it has flowered indoors. Set the Easter lily out among herbaceous perennials such as chrysanthemums, phlox, peonies, or, best of all, other lilies. It may flower again the following autumn, and it is almost certain to flower the summer after that and for many summers to come. An Easter lily blooming its snowy white head off among the pinks, reds, purples, and yellows of a mixed flower border is a glorious sight and a lovely reminder of last year's Easter holiday.

In spring, after danger of frost has passed, select a well-drained site in your garden. A spot that receives bright morning sun and partial shade during the afternoon is perfect. If the soil is heavy, add some organic matter, such as peat moss or leaf mold. It is also a good idea to add a slow-release organic fertilizer, such as steamed bonemeal, to the planting hole.

Remove the plant from its container, being extremely careful not to damage the roots. Set the Easter lily 2–3 inches deeper than it was placed in its container. Since the Easter lily is less hardy than most other bulbs, it will benefit from being placed deeper in the earth where it is warmer. After planting, cut the lily back to half its size and water well. Afterwards, irrigate during dry spells.

In late autumn, mulch your plant heavily, especially where winters are severe. Wood chips, pine boughs, and dry leaves are great for keeping the ground warm and preventing the bulb from being heaved out of position from the alternate freezing and thawing of the soil during winter. At some point during the autumn the foliage will wither, as with any other perennial. In spring new leaves should appear, and the plant will bloom in summer.

CALCEOLARIA & CINERARIA

A Dramatic Duo

Scientific Name: *Calceolaria herbeohybrida*
Origin: Andes Mountains

Scientific Name: *Senecio cruentus*
Origin: Canary Islands

These two dramatic and novel plants are botanically unrelated, yet the similarity of their cultural requirements warrant joint treatment in this book. The calceolaria belongs to the figwort family, which also includes the mullen, a common roadside wild flower, as well as the familiar snapdragon and foxglove of English-garden fame. The cineraria is a member of the composite family and a relative of the daisy, dandelion, and chrysanthemum.

Despite their botanical distance, these two plants have some important characteristics in common. Both are raised from seed for spring sales; both require low temperatures to stay fresh as long as possible; both are treated as annuals and discarded after their flowers fade—and the sight of either in full bloom is a treat you will not soon forget.

The calceolaria bears large, slightly hairy, soft leaves, up to 6 inches long, on plants usually less than 1 foot high. The unusual pouch-like flowers, about 2 inches across, are produced in a stunning bouquet above the foliage. Calceolaria blossoms are reminiscent of a lady's handbag, hence their most popular nickname, pocketbook plant, and they are as soft as Italian suede. Flower colors include red, pink, maroon, bronze, and yellow—the latter being the most frequently seen. They are often speckled with brown, purple, or red. I cannot think of a more special gift plant or one more likely to delight its recipient than a calceolaria.

Cinerarias also bear hairy leaves, 3–4 inches long, that are green on top and gray-purple below, on plants about 1 foot high. They produce a glorious massed head of rich-colored, daisy-like flowers above the foliage. The flowers, 1–4 inches across, may be white or the richest shades of pink, red, blue, or violet, often contrasted by white centers. They are gorgeous.

Availability

Both calceolarias and cinerarias are cool growers requiring low temperatures to flower properly. Therefore, they are raised commercially during fall and winter for sales during spring or before. Calceolarias are most available around the Easter holidays, though plants may be found as late as Mother's Day. I have seen them at other seasons, but the best selection is found around Easter, so I would stick with these. Cinerarias are most often found in the shops from January through April.

Selection

When buying either of these plants, select a specimen with plenty of flowers still to open, so the peak of perfection will be reached at home, not in the shop. Most of the calceolarias and cinerarias available are in pretty good shape, but there are a few problems to keep an eye out for.

• Calceolarias are prone to a yellowing of the leaf tips resulting from inadequate soil drainage, too much water, or over fertilizing.

• Stem rot, resulting from plants being potted too deep, poor drainage, or overwatering can also be a problem, so before you buy, check the base of the plant for soft spots.

• Aphids, spider mites, and especially whiteflies are crazy about both plants; watch for these pests, described in Part 5.

• Beware of drooping plants potted in well-moistened soil, a symptom of wilt disease, to which cinerarias are subject.

Cultural Requirements

The care of calceolarias and cinerarias is remarkably similar, as are the cultural mistakes made with them. The most common error is keeping these cool growers in too warm a spot, a condition guaranteed to cause their speedy and heartbreaking decline.

LIGHT: Both plants should be placed in bright indirect light while in flower. Too much light will cause the leaves to wilt and turn brown and the flowers to fade.

TEMPERATURE: Night temperatures of 40–45° F. and day temperatures of 55–60° F. are perfect. Set these plants in a very cool spot, such as an entranceway, unheated porch, or cool bay window.

MOISTURE: Water both plants thoroughly when the top layer of soil feels dry to the touch. Since calceolarias and cinerarias tend to dry very quickly between waterings, check daily to see if irrigation is required. Avoid splashing water on the foliage; fuzzy leaves spot easily. Keep water off calceolaria flowers—they also tend to spot. To avoid stem rot, never pour water into the center of either plant. Instead, place the spout of your watering can just inside the rim of the pot.

FERTILIZER: These plants do not require fertilizer while in bloom.

PLACEMENT IN THE HOME: Avoid placing these plants in drafty areas. Appropriately low temperatures are mandatory, however; placement of these plants in a cool room is essential to their endurance.

After Flowers Fade

Now for the darker side of the calceolaria/cineraria story. Both of these plants are, from a practical point of view, annuals. They are grown from seed for winter or spring bloom and then discarded. To try and carry them over is a colossal waste of time and energy. There is no comparison in quality between a seed-grown plant and one dragged over from one Easter to the next. I know it is hard to toss out once-glorious plants, but after the flowers die, out they must go. Do not make this any more difficult than discarding a bunch of week-old, faded cut flowers.

Growing Plants from Seed

The germinating requirements for both calceolarias and cinerarias are a bit tricky, so I do not recommend growing either from seed unless you have a greenhouse, or a fluorescent light fixture, plus some experience in seed propagation. However, if you choose to give it a try, here are a few tips that will make your job easier.

• To have grown flowering plants by Easter, sow seeds by July 15. Since growth is more rapid in a greenhouse, plants raised there should be started by September 1.

• Obtain a sterilized germinating medium and a sterilized germinating container. Milled sphagnum moss in a seed flat or clay pot will do perfectly. Since damping off, a disease affecting seeds and seedlings (described in Part 5), is a common problem with both of these plants, clean equipment is a must.

• Follow the instructions for kalanchoes on page 87 for germinating seeds except for the following points: Keep the planted seeds in a cool room, around 50° F.; transplant seedlings as soon as they can be handled to avoid post-emergence damping off; do not pot seedlings too deep, a common cause of stem rot; keep young plants in a spot where temperatures are 48–58° F.; shelter plants from direct light, except during winter when they need all the light they can get; repot plants as soon as needed— ultimately they should be in 4–5-inch containers; give young plants the same treatment as that described under "Cultural Requirements," page 27.

CALADIUM

Fancy Foliage

Scientific Name: *Caladium* species
Origin: Hybrid

Show me any other leaves as exotic and colorful as a caladium's, and I'll show you a rex begonia. When it comes to foliage, these two are in a class by themselves. Yet unlike the rexes, which are fussy and demanding, caladiums are easy to grow and fairly tolerant of adversity, traits which belie their delicate appearance. Caladiums were the first plants I ever grew from scratch. I love them as much now as I did all those years ago when they thrived so valiantly on a dreary city windowsill at the hands of a beginner.

Caladium leaves come in combinations of red, pink, silver, orange, white, and green, depending on which of the dozens of hybrids you buy. The leaves are arrow-shaped, up to 24 inches long, and are produced on stalks up to 18 inches high that arise from the soil in clusters. They feel like onion-skin paper and, because of their size, remind some folks of elephants' ears, their most common nickname.

People are often surprised to learn that caladiums are related to philodendrons. They belong to the aroid family, a fascinating group of tropical plants which produce blossoms composed of a leaf-like spathe holding a knobby column called a spadix. Unlike their more common relatives, caladiums grow from tubers 1½– 2½ inches long and require a dormant period during which their leaves completely die back. However, since they stay in top form for months and are so beautiful between rests, the patience required to get them started and then restarted after dormancy is more than justified.

Availability

Full-grown caladiums are often sold throughout spring and early summer. At this stage they make irresistible gift plants. Caladium tubers, the bulb-like structures from which the plants grow, are also sold during spring and summer for garden bedding or growing in pots for windowsill display. There are also newly started plants sold in trays, just like annuals, for planting in the summer garden—a more expensive purchase than unstarted tubers, but a head start on the growing season. A wonderful selection of tubers can be found through the mail order companies, several of which are listed in the appendix.

Selection

Unfortunately, I often come across caladiums that have passed their prime. These plants do not seem to ship at all well and sometimes decline quickly during transit. To avoid a plant that is on its way out, look for plenty of leaves still curled up at the base—not one on which all the foliage has unfurled. The larger the furled leaf, the larger the open blade, so look for generously sized new growth. Also, foliage colors should be clear and bright, not faded or scorched. Keep an eye out for the usual house plant pests, though caladiums are relatively trouble-free.

Cultural Requirements

Follow these tips whether you have acquired a full-grown plant or have grown one yourself from a tuber.

LIGHT: Provide the caladium with bright indirect light. Too much sun will cause the leaves to fade; not enough will result in weak, floppy growth. Your plant should stand up straight.

TEMPERATURE: Night temperatures of 60–70° F. and day temperatures up to 85° F. are ideal. The caladium is the plant for a warm apartment or over-heated room.

MOISTURE: Water thoroughly when the top layer of soil in the container feels dry to the touch. Be sure to discard any excess moisture that accumulates in the drip plate beneath the container. Tubers rot easily if the soil is kept soggy, so be sure not to irrigate more frequently than necessary.

FERTILIZER: Caladiums that are fully or almost fully grown do not require fertilizer. Newly planted tubers and partially grown specimens do, as described under "Growing Caladiums from Tubers," page 31.

PLACEMENT IN THE HOME: One of the loveliest plant displays I have ever seen included only members of the aroid family. Caladiums were in the center and served as the focal point. In the foreground were green-leaved philo-dendrons and spathiphyllums, both described in Part 4. Try to avoid displaying caladiums near other fancy foliage plants, most of which will pale in comparison to the caladium.

Dormant Period

Regardless of how well your caladium is cared for, within around 6 months the leaves will begin to fade and look rather miserable, a signal that the dormant period is about to begin. When the plant has significantly declined in vigor and appearance, begin "drying off" the tuber by watering less frequently. As the leaves yellow and then turn brown, the plant will look dreadful. Don't worry about this.

Once the leaves have lost all color, cut off the top growth, allow the soil to dry completely, and remove the tuber, the thick knobby structure from which the top growth arose. Put the tuber in an open paper bag filled with dry vermiculite or peat moss and store the bag in a dry place where temperatures are 50–65° F. In 4 or 5 months retrieve the tuber and repot as described in the following section.

Growing Caladiums from Tubers

Plant caladium tubers, indented-side up, about 2 inches below the surface of a 5–6-inch pot filled with equal parts of packaged potting soil and perlite to which about ¼ cup of crushed eggshell has been added. Keep the newly potted tuber in a warm spot, 70° F. or so, on a bright windowsill.

Water thoroughly when the top soil layer feels dry to the touch. Fertilize every 2 weeks with a water-soluble chemical fertilizer, analysis of 20–20–20, at one-half the strength suggested on the label. The tubers take up to 2 months to begin growing, so be patient. People often think nothing is going to happen, but trust that sooner or later you will see the first tightly furled leaf poke through the soil surface. Once it does, things will start to happen pretty fast.

Continue to provide the same care. When the plant produces a flower, cut it off; the bloom is unattractive and takes energy from the spectacular foliage. In addition, the flower smells unpleasant. It is no loss.

Once the plant is fully grown, provide the same care as described under "Cultural Requirements," page 30. You can repeat this process for several years. Each season the tuber will grow larger and produce a fuller, more lovely specimen.

Caladium tubers can be planted out in the garden when the ground warms up in late spring. Partially shaded areas like those in which impatiens, coleus, and wax begonias thrive are perfect for caladiums. So, if you have tired of the more standard, shade-loving fare, give caladiums a try. Of course, the tubers, which are not hardy in colder climates, must be dug and stored as described under "Dormant Period," page 30, before the first hard autumn frost.

To get a head start on the growing season, you can start tubers indoors as soon as they become available and plant them outside when the ground warms up—say 2 or 3 weeks after the last frost.

PRIMROSE

For Gift and Garden

Scientific Name: *Primula* species
Origin: Orient

Among the multitude of dubious horticultural clichés is one with which I genuinely agree: "Primroses are the harbingers of spring."

On a commercial level, the striking flowers of the hardy, shade-loving polyantha primrose (*Primula polyantha*) make quite a popular gift plant. They are sold not only as garden plants, but also as potted specimens for holiday giving. They bear flowers in a wonderfully wide range of colors, either solid or variegated, including white, yellow, pink, red, rose, apricot, lavender, and purple. Flowers are about 2 inches across and are produced on 6–12-inch stalks above the foliage. The rough-textured leaves, about 1 foot long, are produced in a low-growing rosette. This plant blooms naturally in May, but is forced by the professionals to flower during Easter and before. The polyantha primrose is a perennial, hardy in zones 3 to 8, where it can be permanently planted outdoors after its flowers fade. The Pacific Giant strain of polyantha primroses is the "in" group of primroses and well worthy of a place in any garden. Yet polyantha primroses are not the only hybrids sold for gift giving; as a group, primroses have become a profitable crop for commercial growers.

The fairy primrose (*Primula malacoides*) also is one of the more popular species. It bears tufts of flowers less than 1 inch across, in white and shades of pink, red, or lilac, held above the foliage on plants up to 1½ feet high. Its long-stalked, oval leaves are about 3 inches long. Varieties belonging to the Rhinepearl series, with clear, colored flowers born close to the foliage, are among the finest plants of this species. The fairy primrose is an annual plant raised in commercial greenhouses for winter and spring sales. It is generally discarded after the flowering period.

The obconica or top primrose (*Primula obconica*) bears clusters of fragrant blossoms about 1 inch across, in red, pink, lavender, and white. Its hairy leaves, about 4 inches long, are produced on plants about 1 foot high. The leaves and flowers of this species may cause a poison-ivy-like skin rash on contact. Needless to say, these primroses are less popular as living gifts than most plants. The obconica primrose is a perennial, but it is usually handled like an annual and discarded after it has finished blooming.

Availability

All three of these primroses are found in shops from around the first of the year through early spring. I would stick with those available around Easter time—not the plants heavily forced for midwinter bloom. Those that flower closer to their natural time seem to adjust more readily to life indoors and generally hold up longer.

Selection

Select a healthy-looking plant with green leaves; yellowing of the foliage indicates overly acid soil, overwatering, a fertilizer imbalance, or pesticide damage. Make sure there are plenty of flowers yet to open after purchase. Watch out for leaf spots, indicating one of various fungi, and a mosaic pattern on the foliage, indicating viral infection. Also, keep an eye out for aphids, mealybugs, and spider mites.

Cultural Requirements

You need to follow only a few simple tips to get the most from your primrose during the blooming period.

LIGHT: Bright indirect light is recommended. Placement on a northern windowsill or in front of a sunnier window where light is diffused by sheer curtains, partially closed shutters, or shrubs growing in front of the window should do nicely.

TEMPERATURE: Night temperatures of 40–50° F. and day temperatures of 68° F. or lower are ideal. Primroses may decline rapidly if temperatures are too high.

MOISTURE: Water thoroughly when the top soil layer in the container feels dry to the touch. Wait about 15 minutes and discard the excess moisture that accumulates in the drip plate beneath the pot.

FERTILIZER: Primroses do not require fertilizer while in bloom.

PLACEMENT IN THE HOME: As with other plants that require low temperatures, the primroses can be moved from the cool growing area when you are entertaining, as long as they are returned to the growing area in due course.

After Flowers Fade

After the flowers of the fairy and obconica primroses fade, the plants should be discarded. Though the latter is actually a perennial, carrying it over is extremely difficult and not worth the trouble; be brave and toss it out. The polyantha primrose is another matter. If you live in zones 3 to 8, the plant can be set out in the garden as a permanent part of your collection. Its bright flower colors will make a wonderful addition to the early spring garden, complementing the spring flowering bulbs beautifully.

Sometime after the ground has thawed in spring, select a moist, well-drained spot in a partially shaded area. Dig some leaf mold into the soil. Unpot and plant the primrose at approximately the same depth it was set in its container. Mulch the primrose after planting to keep the soil cool and moist. Re-mulch before winter to protect it from the elements.

Propagation

The polyantha primrose is propagated by division every few years. The plant is dug up, split in half or in sections, and replanted exactly the way other garden perennials are divided. Besides providing a source of material for future gift giving, this will keep plants flowering well.

PART 2

Autumn Extravaganza

A Glorious Trio of Living Gifts

To plant lovers, autumn means more than the beauty of sugar maple leaves at their peak of color, or pyracantha spilling over with bright orange fruit. It marks the beginning of the end of the gardening season in most parts of the country. Some people who take pleasure in tending a garden probably find this a sad time. I do not.

By mid-fall I have had enough of planting, pruning, mowing, weeding, raking, mulching, rearranging, staking, and tying. I have had enough of bug bites, dirty fingernails, tangled hoses, and soiled clothes. I am pooped and want nothing more than to amble through the woods and take in the show created by nature's effort, not my own. Winter brings a much-needed rest and time for my annual fantasy search through garden catalogs, a renewed interest in long-neglected house plants, and pipedreams of next year's inspired and sure-to-be-sensational garden designs. I love it.

Sometime before the last spring bulb has been planted, the last leaf raked off the lawn, and the last chrysanthemum cut for indoor arranging, I bring the house plants that have spent the summer outside back indoors for the winter. I check them carefully for insects. Invariably, a few are hosting aphids or spider mites, and I treat them accordingly. Most need repotting after their flush of summer growth, a phenomenon I am always surprised by. Many have outgrown their old places inside the house, and new arrangements must be worked out to accommodate what are no longer windowsill-sized specimens. I usually give a few away to avoid the interior tropical-rainforest motif which has become so popular in urban bars and restaurants. It isn't suitable for a life style that includes small children. As a result of this forced generosity, my autumn plant gifts are often rather dramatic, if not a bit gaudy. But I've had no complaints so far.

Foliage plants that are lush and gorgeous from a summer outdoors make great gifts for autumn. But if you want something in bloom, something with pizzazz, chrysanthemums are your best bet. There are other choices, to be sure, including gloxinias and African violets, but the mum is most closely associated with this season, despite its year-round availability, and it is always welcomed. Potted or cut, chrysanthemums are found in a mind-boggling array of colors and types—they are perfect to bring to Thanksgiving dinner hosts. You can buy potted plants or cut flowers almost everywhere during fall. Potted specimens can be imaginatively wrapped, just like Christmas plants, as described on page 58.

Amaryllis bulbs also fill the marketplace during autumn. In bloom, they have no rival for color and panache. You can present a newly potted bulb that the recipient will have no trouble bringing into bloom as long as a few simple requirements are met. You can also bring the amaryllis into bloom yourself and present it sometime during winter. Flowering time depends on the potting date—amaryllis bloom around 8 weeks after planting. Of course, this requires a bit of long-range planning, but it can be well worth it.

The hardy Dutch bulbs—daffodils, tulips, and hyacinths—make unusual autumn gifts. These bulbs are normally planted in the garden during autumn and bloom the following spring. However, they can be forced to bloom indoors in late winter when planted in a container during fall, then given a long cold period outdoors or in a cool cellar, followed by a warm spell inside. An autumn gift of newly potted bulbs does not offer the instant gratification of a flowering chrysanthemum plant, but when accompanied by instructions on how to force them into bloom, bulbs make a lovely present. (The instructions could be printed on decorative note paper.) Another alternative is to provide the bulbs with the necessary cold period yourself, bring them into bloom, and present these beauties in all their glory during late winter. This task really separates the wheat from the chaff when it comes to planning and organization. Regardless of the stage at which you present hardy bulbs, they are worthwhile gift choices, and when in bloom they bring the aura of spring into the dead of winter.

Though the plant gifts associated with fall are fewer than those available at other seasons, quality makes up for quantity. There may not be an autumn cornucopia of choices, but chrysanthemums, amaryllis, and the hardy bulbs make a glorious threesome for gift giving from September through the start of the Christmas holidays.

CHRYSANTHEMUMS

Queens of Autumn

Scientific Name: *Chrysanthemum morifolium*
Origin: Orient

If a word-association test were given to an old-time plant lover, the clue "chrysanthemum" would surely elicit the response "autumn flower." Modern growers are more likely to say "a plant for all seasons," since mums, once available almost exclusively during fall, their natural blooming period, are now found in shops year-round. Ever responsive to the marketplace, commercial growers use artificial lights or hang black cloth over plants to imitate autumn's day length and force mums into bloom at any season. Nowadays, you are just as likely to find the potted Queens of Autumn in April as you would at Thanksgiving.

If you are looking for a splashy gift with excellent indoor-keeping qualities, mums should fill the bill. There are several types available in a wide color range, so you are certain to find the perfect choice.

Description

Chrysanthemums are members of the composite family, one of the largest groups of flowering plants. The composites bear what resembles a single blossom but is really a compact floral head made up of hundreds of individual flowers known as "florets." The florets look just like petals. Asters, dandelions, black-eyed susans, daisies, and sunflowers are also members of the composite family and have similar floral structures.

The different nonbotanical categories of chrysanthemums can be a source of great confusion. I will try to keep things simple by explaining and describing four common ways that mums are grouped: 1) flower color, 2) structure and arrangement of florets, 3) method of pruning, and 4) blooming date.

The most prominent chrysanthemum feature is obviously *flower color*. The National Chrysanthemum Society, Inc., recognizes five color classes: white, yellow, purple-pink, bronze-orange, and red. Bicolored forms are also common. Flower and plant size vary, but most pot specimens are about 30 inches high and bear flowers 3–4 inches across.

The Society also groups mums by the *structure and arrangement of florets.* The four types most commonly grown in pots are decorative, single, spider, and anemone-flowered chrysanthemums. The decoratives constitute the overwhelming majority of pot plants. For the most part, when you see large stocks of potted mums for sale, particularly in super-markets, they are decoratives. Their outer florets are longer than those in the middle and the "flower" is more or less flattened. Single mums are the up-and-coming type for pot culture. Their florets are arranged around a flattened disk of what are actually shorter florets. They closely resemble daisies and are, in fact, nicknamed daisy mums. The dramatic and exotic spider mums are named for their long, thin, tubular florets. They are my favorites, but, unfortunately, they are a bit more difficult to come by. Anemone mums are similar to singles but have longer disk florets and more closely resemble garden anemones.

Mums are also grouped by the *method of pruning*, regardless of floral structure. On most pot mums, the plant's side shoots are removed, and only one flower is allowed to develop at the tip of each stem. This practice is called "disbudding" and results in fewer and larger flowers produced in a canopy above the foliage. Other pot mums are called "sprays." They are grown so that some or all of the lateral buds are allowed to develop, resulting in three to five smaller flowers per stem. It is easy to recognize which pruning method was used on your plant.

Finally, chrysanthemums are divided into two general groups based on *flowering dates*. There are garden mums, which have a natural blooming time from late August through September. In areas where the first frost is in early or mid-October, the plants bloom before the flowers can be damaged by below-freezing temperatures. There are also greenhouse mums, which bloom naturally from around late September through October. If planted outdoors, the flowers will certainly be killed should the first frost arrive during that time. Of course, exact blooming dates vary depending on the variety of chrysanthemum and the environmental conditions.

The distinction between garden and greenhouse mums is important if you intend to plant your gift outdoors in the spring. A greenhouse mum cannot be left outdoors in an area where the first frost comes in early October, or the flowers will be blackened by the cold. However, if the plant is only to be used for interior decoration until the flowers fade and then discarded, this difference is of little consequence.

Selection

Before purchasing a chrysanthemum plant, give it the once-over. Check to see that there are healthy leaves down to the bottom of each stem. If lower leaves have become dry, there may be a foliage disease, micro-scopic plant parasites may be present, or there may have been a cultural error—probably overwatering. This condition may also indicate that the plant was grown in overcrowded conditions.

If you are buying plants off-season, carefully check the flowers for readiness. The blooms should be fully or almost fully opened. Buds that are just beginning to show color or are only partly opened may not fully develop indoors, though this seems to be less of a problem during autumn. Naturally, you want the flowers on a newly purchased plant to look as fresh as possible, not in the least faded.

Though most chrysanthemums found in the shops are trouble-free and picture-perfect, occasionally you will find a less than healthy specimen offered for sale. Mums attract a wide variety of pests. Aphids are a fairly common chrysanthemum visitor and can cause severe disfiguration if infestation is heavy; mealybugs, also quite prevalent, may be found at the point where a leaf joins the stem; spider mites are one of the worst chrysanthemum enemies and may infest both leaves and flowers; and whitefly, a true mum lover, can be detected by gently shaking the plant, causing these insects to take flight—you can't miss them.

Several diseases also affect mums, including powdery mildew, wilt, fungus leaf spot, stem rot, and flower blight (see Part 5). If you familiarize yourself with these maladies, their signs and symptoms can be easily detected and you will have no trouble avoiding the purchase of a sick plant.

Most chrysanthemums that I see offered for sale are not labeled, so you don't know if you are buying a garden mum or a greenhouse mum. Since this fact can be an important determinant of how you will handle and present the plant, try to find out from the shopkeeper which type he is selling. If he does not know (not an unusual occurrence), I would treat the plant as if it were a greenhouse type. Keep in mind, though, that garden mums are most often sold during fall.

Cultural Requirements

The care of a newly purchased flowering mum is similar to that of poinsettias, cyclamens, and many other gift plants. The difference comes after the plant has flowered. At that point, a decision must be made either to discard the mum, to plant it outdoors during spring for fall flowering, to plant it outdoors to be dug in autumn for indoor display, or to try to carry it over indoors—undoubtedly the most challenging option.

LIGHT: To keep flowers fresh for the longest period of time, keep newly acquired mums out of direct sun and provide bright filtered light for about 4 hours each day.

TEMPERATURE: Night temperatures of 45–55° F. and day temperatures below 68° F. will help prolong flower freshness and keep your display in top form for several weeks.

MOISTURE: Water potted mums thoroughly when the top layer of soil in the container feels dry to the touch. You may find that potted mums dry more quickly between waterings than many other plants—check often.

FERTILIZER: It is not necessary to fertilize chrysanthemums while they are in bloom. Plants have been kept on a rigorous fertilizing schedule by the grower who raised them, and they need no additional nutrients at this time.

PLACEMENT IN THE HOME: Obviously, you should place the mum where it will benefit from appropriate temperatures and light intensity. However, such a spot is unlikely to be where the plant looks best. Feel free to move your mum to a coffee table or set it on the mantle during evening or while entertaining. No harm will be done. For temporary displays, mums look sensational grouped with foliage plants or other flowering plants in complementary colors. Try creating this type of grouping in front of your fireplace, on a dining room buffet, or on the floor in a corner of your living room. Just remember to put the mum back in a cool, indirectly lit spot within a day or two.

After Flowers Fade

Regardless of how mums are handled after flowering, blossoms should be cut once they have faded. Many people toss out the chrysanthemum at this point as they would a bunch of cut flowers. If you cannot bear to discard a once-beautiful gift and want to try your hand at carrying it over, read on.

PLANTING GARDEN MUMS OUTDOORS: After the chrysanthemum flowers fade, prune the plant back to half its size, place it on a windowsill that receives some direct sunlight, water thoroughly whenever the top soil layer feels dry, fertilize every month with a water-soluble chemical fertilizer high in phosphorus (such as a product with an analysis of 15–30–15), and maintain temperatures around 65° F.

After the last frost, likely in mid-spring, the chrysanthemum can be planted outdoors. Mums are perennial, and their natural flowering time is autumn. They die back to the ground during winter and begin growing again in early spring. Mums should be planted in a sunny, well-drained spot where the soil has been enriched with organic matter such as peat moss or compost. They are a snap to grow, requiring little more than division every other year during spring and some slow-release, high-phosphorus, dry fertilizer *every* spring. A liquid feed applied every few weeks from spring through summer can be substituted for the dry fertilizer.

Early each summer I prune my mums to half their size—a practice that encourages a low bushy habit, helps avoid the need for staking, and prevents plants from coming into bloom too early. I want my mums to bloom in September when garden color and cut flowers for indoor arrangements are at a premium—not in August, which they are apt to do if left un-pruned. In winter, after the stems have died back, cut off the above-ground parts and cover the crown with a thick mulch of dry leaves, pine boughs, or wood chips for protection.

PLANTING GREENHOUSE MUMS OUTDOORS: If you have received a greenhouse mum, the care after flowering is the same as described for garden mums. The difference comes in spring when the mum is planted outdoors, if you live in an area where the first frost is in October or before. In that case, a different type of planting site must be selected. These plants tend to bloom from late September through October, after the first frost hits colder areas, and the flowers can be killed by low temperatures. If you can plant your mum in a protected area near the house or near a windbreak, the flowers may be spared any cold damage. If you live in a warmer part of the country, you have no problem, since the first autumn frost comes later than the flowering period of greenhouse chrysanthemums.

If you cannot protect a greenhouse mum from low autumn temperatures, dig the plant up before the first frost and pot it for indoor decoration. Mums take to this treatment very well. To successfully transfer mums from the garden to containers for indoor display follow these suggestions:

• By the time you are ready to dig up your mum, there should be color showing in the flower buds.
• Water the plant well the day before digging.
• Select a container that is about 10 inches deep and approximately the same diameter as the plant.
• Dig out around the mum in a circle with a radius of 4–6 inches, depending on the size of the plant. Then dig under the root ball—about 8 inches down.
• After placing the freshly dug plant in the pot, fill in any gaps between the inner pot walls and the root ball with fresh soil.
• Firmly tap the pot several times against a hard surface to eliminate any air holes between the root ball and the container.
• Place the newly potted plant in a shady area outdoors and water well.
• Some leaves are likely to yellow within a few days after potting—simply remove them.
• The stems may require staking to stay upright in their new container. Bamboo stakes and green twisties will do the job beautifully.
• Water as needed.
• After the plant has been in a shady spot for about a week, move it to a sunnier area. If the mum wilts, return it to the shade and try again in a few days.
• Leave the mum outdoors in a protected area until just before the first frost. You should see lots of color in the buds at this point.

- Move the plant indoors before the first frost.
- When it is inside, maintain night temperatures of 50–60° F. to prolong flower freshness.
- Continue to water as needed. Fertilizer is not necessary.

GROWING MUMS YEAR-ROUND INDOORS: The only way for a gardenless gardener to carry over a chrysanthemum after the flowers have faded is to grow it indoors on a windowsill. I do not recommend this process because it is time consuming, difficult, and a real pain in the neck. However, the more adventurous and dedicated among you may wish to try.

Initial Care

- After flowers fade, cut them off and prune your plant to half its original size.
- Place the plant on a windowsill that gets several hours of direct sunlight. At this point you want the mum to cease flowering and begin producing new foliage, a condition that will occur only when days are long and nights short. The reading lights and television sets that are normally left on after dark will provide enough additional light to hood-wink your mum into responding as if days were long.
- During this time water thoroughly whenever the top layer of soil in the container feels dry, and fertilize every 2 weeks with a water-soluble chemical fertilizer high in phosphorus.
- After there has been a flush of new growth, take cuttings that are 3–4 inches long. They should be as uniform in size as possible. Make the cuts just above the point where the leaf is attached to the stem.

Rooting Cuttings

- Cuttings can be rooted in a clear plastic box filled halfway to the top with moistened vermiculite, exactly as described for kalanchoes on page 87. Chrysanthemum cuttings root easily in a few weeks. After there is a healthy mass of 2-inch roots, pot five cuttings in a 6-inch pot filled with a mixture of 2 parts packaged potting soil and 1 part perlite. Plant the cuttings around the perimeter of the container. They should be planted at the same depth as they were in the propagating box. It is best to place the cuttings at an angle so the tops extend slightly over the edge of the pot and the middle is left open to admit light and air. This arrangement results in superior growth and a more desirable form.
- Set the newly potted cuttings on a windowsill in direct sunlight. Optimum temperatures at this time are 60–65° F.
- Water when the top layer of soil in the container feels dry. Set pots on a pebble tray to keep the humidity high and prevent the leaves from turning crisp around the edges.

• After the cuttings have developed several new leaves, pinch off the top half-inch to force new growth from the base. Ideally, there should be about ten leaves on each stem below the pinch. Pinching is essential to promote branching and develop a multi-stemmed specimen. A few weeks after pinching, the plant will be ready for the short-day treatment crucial to flower formation.

Short Days

• Mums bloom only when the days are short and nights are long. The number of short days a mum requires to begin blooming depends on variety. The fastest flowering types respond to short days by flowering in 7 weeks, the slowest take 15 weeks—9-, 10-, and 11-week varieties are used most often for pot culture.

• The daily dark period must be 12 to 15 hours long. This will require you to place your plant in the dark for that period each day until flower buds are well formed and show color. I describe how to provide a dark period for poinsettias on page 65; the principles are exactly the same for mums. The plant must be given direct sunlight between the dark periods and watered as needed.

• During the short-day treatment, night temperatures of 60–65° F. should be maintained. However, once color appears in the buds, night temperatures of 55° F. will improve plant quality. Cool temperatures are also required for the poinsettia, and the advice for providing those low temperatures can be applied to the chrysanthemum.

• If you want to disbud your mum to produce one large flower at each stem tip as opposed to several small blossoms per stem, allow the uppermost bud on each stem to develop and remove all side buds as soon as they appear. If you prefer a spray mum, allow the top three or four buds to develop and promptly pinch off the rest. You will get a greater number of smaller flowers. Size or quantity? You decide.

This entire routine can be repeated year after year and can result in a bumper crop of chrysanthemums for decorating or giving. Enjoy the extravaganza!

AMARYLLIS

The Dazzler

Scientific Name: *Hippeastrum* hybrids
Origin: Southern Africa

If your list of desirable traits in flowering house plants starts with drama and ends with subtlety, the amaryllis should suit you to a tee. The proper name for these bulbs is *Hippeastrum*, a word which seems to hint at the size of the flowers and the bulb from which they grow. The enormous, bold-colored blossoms of the amaryllis, generally produced in winter, would catch the eye of Mr. Magoo from across the ballroom at the Waldorf. Though this plant may not be admired for its reserve, it surely cannot be ignored.

Description

The amaryllis, like the paperwhites described on page 50, is a "tender bulb." It will not survive winters outdoors except in zone 9. Generally speaking, if you live anywhere other than Florida or southern California, the amaryllis is strictly a house plant.

Amaryllis flower colors include white, various pinks and lavenders, shades of red, including the richest reds imaginable, and some extraordinary bicolors—red and white among the showiest. The trumpet-shaped blossoms, usually 4–8 inches wide, have five petals and are produced in a group of four (though sometimes only two or three blossoms appear simultaneously) on thick stems about 2 feet high. The anthers, threadlike structures produced in the center of the flower, bear bright yellow pollen which contrasts strikingly with the petal color.

The amaryllis is among the easiest bulbs to grow. Unlike the "hardy bulbs," such as tulips, daffodils, and hyacinths, it requires no cold period before blooming. In fact, a newly purchased bulb is almost guaranteed to bloom if properly potted and provided with a few basics. As far as bulbs are concerned, it is about as foolproof as you can get.

There you have it: bright and flashy flowers in a wide assortment of bold colors on plants that are a snap to grow. What's the hitch? Unfortunately, it's price. An amaryllis bulb can be frightfully expensive, up to $25 per bulb—much more than a hyacinth or a handful of daffodils. But the plant can be forced to bloom again and again with a minimum of effort and without the irritating proviso of a cold period required by hardy bulbs,

44

which is difficult to provide if you live in an apartment. Also, the amaryllis is fairly easily propagated, so your initial investment offers dividends in the form of new plants produced from the original purchase which can become gifts in the future.

Availability and Selection

A wide selection of amaryllis bulbs is offered in the fall catalogs of many of the major mail order plant companies that are listed in the appendix. You can order them for giving in autumn, at Christmas, or beyond.

Amaryllis bulbs are generally available in garden centers from October through December. They bloom about 8 weeks after planting, so plan accordingly if you wish to give a budded or blooming specimen. This may be a bit difficult to schedule perfectly since the exact flowering time depends on bulb size, the particular hybrid grown, and conditions inside your home. However, there is no need to worry if you planned to present a flowering amaryllis and the buds are still closed on gift day. The recipient is sure to be just as delighted if the plant is not in its glory until a week or so later. After all, a budding plant foretells a dramatic and showy future. It is certainly better to present the plant a bit early than late—when flowers are beginning to fade. Already-flowering amaryllis plants are occasionally found in the marketplace, but often at prices sufficiently high to cause consumers to faint. I would not dream of purchasing one.

As always, if you shop for an amaryllis by mail, you must trust the source. If you are hand picking bulbs from the garden center, remember that the bigger the bulb, the larger the plant and its flowers. If you wish to spend more modestly, that's fine, too. The amaryllis bulb increases in size with each season, and you will, in essence, grow your own giant-sized bulb in due course. As with other bulbs, select a specimen that is firm all over with no soft or rotten spots.

I have noticed that many of the bulbs offered for sale have already started producing leaves or a flower bud. If the growth has just begun, you have a little head start. However, if growth is several inches high, pick another bulb. An amaryllis which has grown that much before planting has been forced to live off the moisture and nutrients stored inside the bulb—not a good situation.

There are also amaryllis kits offered for sale and featured in many autumn plant catalogs. These kits include the bulb, a container, and an appropriate amount of potting mix. While they make life easy for the recipient, you often end up paying more for the package than you would if you set yourself up from scratch. With amaryllis you would do better to spend your money on a large bulb than a kit, especially since a self-styled kit can be put together less expensively than a commercial one. It also makes a more charming presentation.

Cultural Requirements

There is nothing tricky about planting an amaryllis bulb and getting it to bloom. The challenge is in carrying the bulb over and persuading it to flower the following year. Even this task is not really difficult—no special equipment or conditions are needed. It is just a bit time consuming and requires some perseverance.

PLANTING THE BULB: Place a clay shard or a small piece of wire screening over the drainage hole of a pot that is 1½–2 inches larger in diameter than the widest part of the bulb. The pot may seem a bit snug, but amaryllis grow best in tight containers.

Prepare a growing medium of 2 parts packaged potting soil, 1 part perlite, and approximately 1 tablespoon of a slow-release pellet fertilizer recommended for use on flowering house plants. The fertilizer will help supply the nutrients necessary for the production of next year's blossoms.

Pot the bulb, pointed-end up, so that the top half is above the soil line and the bottom half is below ground. This may seem odd, but bulbs planted this way seem to flower more freely. After potting, water thoroughly until water runs through the drainage holes in the bottom of the pot.

CARE AFTER PLANTING: Place the newly potted bulb on a sunny windowsill in a room where temperatures range between 55 and 65° F. Warmer temperatures may result in growth that is weak and floppy. While flowers will still be produced, staking may be required. Colder temperatures result in sturdier growth.

Water thoroughly whenever the top layer of soil feels dry to the touch. If the soil is kept too wet, the bulb may rot—a constant threat with bulbous plants. As the roots develop and fill the container, the top layer of soil will dry more quickly and the frequency of watering should be increased accordingly.

Leaves may develop first, or the bud may emerge from the side of the bulb before the appearance of foliage. Whether this depends on the hybrid grown or on cultural techniques is uncertain. Regardless of the explanation, once growth begins, give the pot a quarter turn every few days to prevent the plant from leaning toward the light.

If the amaryllis has been grown in a room where temperatures rise above 65° F., the flower stalk may require staking to stay upright. A thin green bamboo stick carefully placed between the bulb and the inner pot wall will do the job unobtrusively. Tie the stem to the stake with green twisties.

After Flowers Fade

Remove the flowers after they have opened and faded, but do not cut off the green flower stalk or any of the foliage. Place the plant back on a sunny windowsill. Continue to water thoroughly when the top layer of soil feels dry to the touch. Frequently, the bulb will send up a second set of blossoms—most likely if you are growing one of the larger bulbs. The second set of flowers may be smaller than the first.

Before you know whether the second flower set will arrive or not, begin fertilizing with a water-soluble chemical fertilizer recommended for use on flowering house plants. Fertilize every month at the strength recommended on the label. This will help supply the bulb with the nutrients needed to produce next year's flowers.

You must then continue to treat the amaryllis as if it were any other house plant with regard to light, water, and fertilizer, until the foliage and the flower stalk yellow naturally. This means keeping it on a sunny windowsill, watering thoroughly when the top layer of soil feels dry to the touch, and fertilizing monthly. If the plant is neglected and allowed to decline prematurely, it may not flower again.

Some folks place the potted amaryllis outdoors during spring, after the danger of frost has passed, and allow the foliage to yellow al fresco. One of the main advantages of this treatment is the removal of the rather undecorative declining amaryllis from the windowsill. Plants set outdoors should be placed where they receive sunlight in the morning and partial shade during the afternoon. While the plant is outdoors, check often to see if watering is needed and continue to fertilize as before until the foliage yellows.

AFTER THE FOLIAGE YELLOWS: The foliage and flower stalk of your amaryllis will stay green throughout spring and will probably turn yellow during summer or early autumn. This depends on the hybrid grown and on your particular conditions. At any rate, once the leaves have yellowed, remove them just above the tip of the bulb. Then store the potted bulb in a place where it will be out of sight (there is nothing attractive about a bare bulb), but not forgotten. A cool place (55–65° F.) such as a basement or a closet that backs onto an outside wall will do perfectly. Just do the best you can to provide such low temperatures during the height of summer.

If the amaryllis was placed outside during summer, bring it back indoors before the first autumn frost. If the foliage has yellowed, remove it and store the potted bulb in a cool basement or closet. If the leaves are still green, place it back on the sunny windowsill and provide the same care as before until yellowing occurs.

Forcing a Second Flowering

The amaryllis requires a 3–4-month cool dry period between the time the foliage yellows and the time you begin the process of forcing it to bloom again. Naturally, the timetable differs depending on environmental conditions and the hybrid grown. Here is one example: An amaryllis planted for the first time in November is likely to be in bloom during January. The leaves will probably be completely yellow by June. The cool dry period could start in June and end in early October. The bulb should flower again in time for the Christmas holidays.

Once the cool dry period has been satisfied, take the potted bulb out of hiding and carefully scrape off the top inch or two of soil. Replace the top of the old medium with fresh mix. Amaryllis do best when their roots are left undisturbed. When repotting, choose a container 1½–2 inches larger in diameter than the widest part of the bulb, which by now will have increased in size.

Water thoroughly. Then place the potted bulb on a sunny windowsill and follow the instructions given under "Care After Planting," page 46.

Propagation

The amaryllis is most easily propagated by separating the offsets or smaller bulbs that develop during the growing season and are attached to the mother bulb. When the offsets are one-fourth to one-third the size of the mother, they can be carefully separated with the fingers or a sharp knife and potted individually. The best time to separate the offsets is after the cool dry period. Since amaryllis grow and flower best when their roots are left undisturbed, propagation is best postponed until repotting time—about every 3 years. When you unpot the bulb for transplanting, you may have one or more offsets of adequate size and you can separate those. In the meantime, the offsets do not harm the mother bulb or impede her flowering, so this job can be delayed. I have seen amaryllis bulbs and their attached offsets blooming simultaneously—quite a glorious sight.

The offsets, like the mother bulb, should be potted in a container that is 1½–2 inches larger in diameter than the widest part of the bulb. Care for the offsets exactly as you would the mother bulb. They probably will not bloom for 2 or 3 years, but you must take them through the same paces as the parent to assure future success.

BULBS

Blooms for an Indoor Spring in Winter

Scientific Name: Various
Origin: Widespread

Few gardening arts provide more satisfaction than forcing spring bulbs to bloom ahead of schedule. Defiance of Mother Nature's plan by providing extravagant blooms for the home is guaranteed to end winter doldrums. You may reasonably wonder why flowers forced for winter bloom are discussed in this section. The explanation is twofold: The best bulbs are available in the fall, and that is when the forcing process begins.

A pot filled with bulbs that you have planted and conditioned for flowering makes a very special, unique, and dramatic gift, yet the cost is less than that of many other flowering plants. Instead of working to ensure a plant's natural flowering schedule, you have the opportunity for greater control over nature's plan. It often turns out that the problem is finding the strength to give away bulbs that promise a spectacular floral show.

Bulbs suitable for forcing can be divided into two general categories: "tender bulbs," those that require no cold period before flowering (though a few weeks in a cool area is recommended for some), and "hardy bulbs," those that must be subjected to many weeks of low temperatures before they will bloom. The former are far easier to grow. In fact, they are almost foolproof. Requirements for the latter are slightly more complex, although the recipe, when carefully followed, almost always turns out a glamorous success.

Bulbs Requiring No Cold Treatment

Bulbs that cannot survive a northern winter outdoors are referred to as tender bulbs. Their need of warm temperatures makes them ideal for successful indoor cultivation. Many of the tender bulbs are conditioned by professional growers to flower ahead of their natural season. Your job is simply to provide a few basic cultural requirements, and—presto—a pot full of flowers.

There is, however, a slight hitch. Many of these bulbs, including the paperwhites, are a one-shot deal. The rigamarole they are put through by professionals to bloom early zaps their strength, and all their remaining energy is channeled into producing one, and only one, set of flowers. I *have* heard tales of growers getting a second set of blooms—by an ela-

49

borate process that sounds like a royal pain. I think it makes far more sense to toss out these bulbs with yesterday's newspapers once they have finished flowering and start over again next year.

PAPERWHITES: The small-flowered *Narcissus* varieties, or daffodils, all of which are known collectively as paperwhites, are the most commonly grown tender bulbs. Three readily available varieties are the Paperwhite (Polyanthus) *Narcissus,* with comparatively large, sweet-scented white flowers; the Soleil d'Or, with golden yellow flowers contrasting a bright orange center "cup"; and the Chinese Sacred Lily, with white flowers and a bright yellow cup. Their cultural requirements are identical and simple.

• Find a shallow bowl, without drainage holes, about 4 inches deep. If you want to use the bulbs as a really serious gift, you may want to purchase a decorative china, delft, or silver bowl (extravagant, I know, but a sensational wedding or anniversary gift).

• Pour pea gravel halfway to the top of the bowl. The gravel, available at garden centers and most hardware stores, serves to anchor the bulbs in place. Neither soil nor fertilizer is required.

• Set the bulbs, pointed-end up, side-by-side, on top of the gravel. Place as many bulbs as possible in the container; the fuller the pot, the more attractive the display. It is no problem if the bulbs are touching.

• Pour water into the bowl up to, but not quite touching, the base of the bulbs.

• Carefully surround the bulbs with more pebbles so they are held firmly in place. The bulbs should just poke up above the pebbles.

• Set the newly potted bulbs in a cool dark spot such as a basement or a cool closet for about 3 weeks. During this time they will develop a root system sufficient to support the top growth that will be produced later.

• Check every week to see if the pebbles beneath the base of the bulbs are dry. If so, add water. Try to prevent the water from coming up to the bulbs—this could cause them to rot.

• After the 3 weeks in a cool basement or closet, place the pot on a sunny windowsill. In about 6 to 8 weeks the bulbs will be in bloom. This period is the perfect time for giving. Assuming a mid-October start, blooms will appear in late January.

• Throughout the blooming period continue to water when the pebbles beneath the base of the bulbs feel dry to the touch—and enjoy.

The pebble method for growing paperwhites is an old standard. Its only drawback is that pebbles will not support wooden stakes should they be required to hold the stems upright as the plants prepare to bloom. You can substitute a mixture of 2 parts moistened peat moss and 1 part perlite for the pebbles. This mix will support stakes to which the stems can be inconspicuously tied with green twisties. Bulbs planted in this mix should be cared for exactly as described for bulbs planted in pebbles.

COLCHICUMS: Another bulb that does not require a cold period, though it is not tender or pretreated, is *Colchicum autumnale major.* Unfortunately, it is nicknamed autumn crocus—which it is not. Forcing the *Colchicums* to bloom is a cinch. Just place the bulb on a windowsill. That's it. You don't need water, soil, or a pot. One *Colchicum* bulb (actually a bulb-like structure called a corm) will produce a succession of blooms in lilac-pink, deep lilac, or lavender, depending on variety, atop stalks about 6 inches high. Flowers appear within a few weeks after the bulbs have been exposed to light and will last a week or more. After flowering, the bulb can be planted in a well-drained part of the garden, where it will bloom again the following fall. *Colchicums* make perfect living gifts for children, who are certain to be fascinated by their magical ability to bloom in very short order and without any assistance.

Bulbs Requiring a Cold Treatment

The "Dutch trio" of hardy bulbs—tulips, daffodils, and hyacinths—forces beautifully indoors. Varieties of all three reward indoor gardeners with displays from January through April, as long as they receive a cold period of sufficient duration—generally 10 to 14 weeks. Planting is most often done between October 1 and December 1. With staggered starting dates, you can have a steady supply of gifts for most of the winter.

Most growers agree that hyacinths are the easiest of the hardy bulbs to force. Medium-sized, trumpet-type daffodils recommended for forcing are in second place. Tulips are considered the most difficult for the novice, though double-flowering tulips (the multi-petaled forms) do somewhat better than the singles. Regardless of which you choose, it is essential to select bulbs *recommended for forcing.* They should be labeled as such either in the plant catalog from which you are shopping or on the display stand at your garden center. Some bulb varieties are far better suited than others for forcing, and making a mistake can be a real drag. Once you have purchased the appropriate stock, here is what to do:

• For planting, obtain what are known as bulb pans, either plastic or clay. They are available through well-supplied garden centers and plant shops. Bulb pans are shallower than standard-sized pots and offer a more pleasing balance between bulbs and container.

• Place a clay shard or small piece of wire screen over the drainage hole in the bottom of the container to prevent soil loss.

• Prepare a potting mixture. There is great controversy over what

makes the best growing medium for bulbs. Equal parts of packaged potting soil, peat moss, and coarse sand or perlite is a widely used mix with
readily available components. Sophisticates prefer what is known as bulb
fiber, a product not widely available and relatively expensive, but very
effective. It is rarely offered in plant shops, but it is sold through a few
mail order companies listed in the appendix. You can make your own version of bulb fiber by mixing 2 parts moistened peat moss, 1 part horticultural
charcoal, and a tablespoon or so of limestone per 6-inch pot. (The limestone counteracts the acidity of the peat.)

• Place bulbs of a single variety in one pot. Bulbs in a mixed planting
are unlikely to bloom simultaneously and often produce an aestheti-
cally confusing display.

• Fill the pot about halfway to the top with the mix.

• Set the bulbs, pointed-end up, on the soil surface—just far enough
apart to prevent them from touching—and very gently twist them into
place. Pot as many bulbs in the pan as will reasonably fit.

• Fill the cracks between each bulb with mix and cover the bulbs so
that just the tip of each is poking through the soil. The soil surface
should be about ½-inch below the pot's rim to allow ample room for
watering.

• Soak thoroughly by pouring water just inside and all around the
rim of the pot, not down through the middle of the bulbs. Some growers
prefer to water from below by letting the pot sit in water until the soil
surface is completely moistened.

• Label each pot with the date planted, as well as the name and color
of the bulbs. When you are ready to present them as gifts, you will know
just what you are giving to whom.

• Check weekly to see if moisture is required. If so, water thoroughly,
until water runs through the drainage holes in the bottom of the container; or, if you have watered from below, until the upper soil surface
is evenly moist.

There are several ways to provide the 10 to 14 weeks of 35–45° F.
temperatures required before these bulbs can be forced into bloom. The
easiest way is to place the pots in an unheated cellar or garage where
temperatures naturally fall within this range. Lower temperatures may
cause the soil to freeze and the bulbs will be ruined. Higher temperatures
will not satisfy the cold requirement.

A cold frame works beautifully for those who have one, although a
window well is a suitable alternative. (What I call a window well is a basement window just below ground level, from which the earth is held back by a
metal bow-shaped well.) Before placing bulbs in a window well, cover
the top of the container with an inverted pot the same size as the one in
which the bulbs are planted. This will protect the plant's stems as they

emerge. Then cover the pots with dry leaves, pine boughs, or styrofoam pellets to prevent the soil from freezing. An alternative to such a cover is a styrofoam cooler that can be set inside the window well. Just place a pot or two of bulbs inside the cooler.

For apartment dwellers, the lowest shelf of your refrigerator might do, though I confess to having only a 50 percent success rate with this method. Apartment dwellers with balconies could try placing potted bulbs in styrofoam coolers covered with pine boughs and set against the building for protection against the cold.

• Whatever method you use, check the pots regularly to see if moisture is required. If so, water thoroughly.

• After the bulbs have been subjected to about 10 weeks of cool temperatures, check to see if there is 2 inches of stem growth. If so, you are ready for the next step. If not, place the pots back in the cool area and check again in a week or so.

• When 2 inches of growth has appeared, place the pots in a room about 60° F., out of direct sunlight, for about 2 weeks, just until the growing tips turn green. Since the tips have developed in the dark, they will start out white.

• Force bulbs into bloom by placing the pots on a sunny windowsill in a room where temperatures are 65–70° F. Higher temperatures may result in growth that is weak and floppy. The forcing period is perfect for gift giving since the recipient can watch as the bulbs come into bloom.

• Continue to water whenever the top layer of potting mix feels very dry to the touch.

• Staking may be required to hold the leaves and flower stalks upright. Thin green bamboo stakes (available in garden centers) and green twisties will do beautifully for this purpose.

Generally, hardy bulbs, like tender ones, can be forced for winter blooming only once. They are then discarded unless you wish to plant them outdoors. If you do, cut off the flowers after they have faded, but leave the green flower stalks and foliage intact. Keep the pots on a sunny windowsill and continue to water when the top soil layer feels dry. The vegetative plant parts (the stalk and the leaves) produce the food to nourish next year's flowers and should be cared for like any other foliage plant with regard to light and water until they yellow naturally. That is, they should be placed on a windowsill that receives some direct sunlight, watered when the top layer of soil in the container feels dry to the touch, and fertilized about once a month with a water-soluble chemical fertilizer recommended for use on house plants. Given this treatment, the leaves will yellow and wither slowly and naturally.

When weather permits, unpot the bulbs and plant them outdoors in a well-drained site. Set the bulbs about 1 inch deeper than they were planted in the forcing container. Some folks carefully separate the bulbs, but they seem to do best when they are unpotted and planted as a group— just as they were arranged in the container. Bulbs transferred outdoors should bloom the second spring after forcing and for several years to come. The hardy bulbs surely offer the renewable pleasures inherent in plant gifts.

Availability and Selection

Bulbs are available in the florist and garden shops and through mail order from early autumn through Christmas— or slightly beyond. Obviously, the earlier you start, the more ahead of season your bulbs will bloom.

When mail ordering, you must, of course, trust your source. If you are hand picking bulbs at the local garden center, look for large firm bulbs with no soft or rotten spots. Also, the tunicate (the onionskin-like shell that covers the bulb), which serves as protection for the bulbs, should be intact. Avoid bulbs with tiny offsets— baby bulbs attached to the mother. These will produce foliage only. However, daffodil or tulip bulbs that are attached, the two bulbs of about equal size, are great because you will probably get two blooms for the price of one.

Storage Before Planting

If you buy all your bulbs at the same time and do not have the opportunity to plant them right away, or you wish to stagger planting dates to get a succession of blooms, the unused bulbs can be stored for about 6 weeks. They should not be left hanging around carelessly, or they will soon dry out or rot, depending on moisture conditions. To maintain the bulbs properly, store them inside a perforated paper bag or net-type potato sack in a dry, cool, dark, well-ventilated spot. Never use plastic. If such a place does not exist, the vegetable crisper in your refrigerator will suffice. Avoid storing bulbs in the light, which may cause them to start growing prematurely.

Growing Accessories

Hyacinth glasses, crocus bowls, and bulb kits, available in increasing quantity and variety, make charming and unusual gifts, especially for children and teens— even if a bit expensive. You can purchase these products through the mail order companies listed in the appendix or from well-supplied garden centers.

HYACINTH GLASSES: Hyacinth glasses are special vases, usually glass, designed for growing hyacinths in water without using any soil. While rather amazing, bulb glasses are nothing new. Hyacinths have been grown in such containers for decades.

The vases are designed so that the bulbs rest on a bowl-shaped ledge at the top and roots grow down through the neck of the container into a flared base. The base is filled with water, and the bottom of the bulb sits ever so slightly above the water. Every few weeks the vase must be checked to see if water needs to be added or if it requires changing. A few pieces of charcoal placed in the bottom of the bulb glass will help keep the water fresh.

Place the bulb glass in a cool basement or in your refrigerator until a heavy mass of roots fills the base and there is 2–3 inches of top growth. This will take about 8 to 12 weeks. Then gradually bring the vase into the sunlight of a bright windowsill.

There are a number of hyacinth varieties recommended for this treatment, and you should stick with them for best results. They can be obtained through the companies listed in the appendix or through large garden centers. There are also crocus vases, which are a smaller version of the hyacinth glass. They are used for giant-flowered crocus varieties and are handled exactly like the hyacinths.

CROCUS BOWLS: Special crocus planters are also offered in the shops and through the mail order companies. The most popular types are more delicate versions of the traditional strawberry jar, usually made of delft, in the Dutch tradition. These bowls have a wide opening at the top and several smaller openings scattered along the sides of the planter. The crocuses are planted so that they gracefully slip through all the openings in the jar as they grow, creating a very pleasant effect. The bowls are generally sold with the appropriate quantity of growing medium, the bulbs themselves, and instructions for planting and forcing the crocuses into flower. The crocuses used in these kits generally bloom 6–7 weeks after planting—a shorter period than that required by the Dutch trio. The same type of bowl is also sold with white or blue scillas (also known as wood hyacinths) substituted for the crocuses.

BULB KITS: There is no end to the types of bulb kits now offered through the mail order plant companies. The kits include some type of container, bulbs (usually crocuses, paperwhites, or hyacinths), an appropriate amount of growing medium, and instructions. Often the bulbs are pretreated so they have to spend less time in a cool area before flowering. This information is provided by the seller. You can have a kit sent by the company directly to the giftee once you have the catalog of the company you wish to do business with.

Kits are a bit trendy, to be sure, and rather costly compared to purchasing the ingredients separately, but they are fun and they make life easy, especially for those who cannot get out to shop for the paraphernalia required.

PART 3

"Tis the Season..."

Christmas Gifts To Last All Year

People have always exchanged plants at Christmas—some folks make it a tradition. December, the beginning of the most colorless period outdoors, produces some of the most vibrant colors and spectacular flowers indoors. The Christmas season offers bright and showy blooms that belie the onset of winter. You cannot go wrong giving someone a beautiful flowering plant at Christmas.

For years I suspected that Christmas plant givers were kindred to people who send gift grams of one sort or another to mark special occasions: that ease and convenience were the main motivations. But giving plants is something quite different. The selection of plants available nowadays is huge. There are as many kinds of plants to select from as there are ties and scarves in department stores, and they are all lovely. You cannot help but become involved in making just the right selection, changing your mind as many times as there are choices.

Beauty and flair in the face of the hostile elements are not the only common characteristics of Christmas plants. Most exhibit what horticulturists call a "short-day" response. Unlike summer bloomers, the natural flowering period for most Yuletide plants occurs when the days are short and the nights are long. The poinsettia provides a classic example. Even if kept on a brightly lit windowsill during the long days of summer and given the royal treatment, a poinsettia will never honor you with a bloom in that season. For flower formation, the day length must be just about 10 hours, as in late fall.

Christmas offerings also share a preference for low temperatures, a fact which should delight economy-minded indoor gardeners. The flowers of the poinsettia, Christmas cactus, Rieger begonia, and most others stay fresh longer when the home is kept at energy-saving temperatures. In fact, most short-day plants are "cool growers." They are raised commercially in greenhouses kept in the 60° F. range. It is easy to understand why professional nurserymen, faced with dramatically escalating fuel costs, are raising Christmas plants in increasingly greater quantities.

Matching Friends with Flowers

Selecting the right plant for the right person requires some forethought. Instead of wondering if a scarf matches your friend's wardrobe, however, with plant gifts the main consideration is the environment in the recipient's home.

Close attention should be paid to the cultural requirements of the plant you purchase. For example, a Christmas cactus requires ample sunlight and is, therefore, unsuitable for someone who lives in a basement apartment or whose windows are shaded by the building next door. The cyclamen, which demands particularly cool temperatures, should not be given to the apartment dweller cursed with an overabundance of dry forced-air heat.

Some plants require careful attention, whereas others are relatively undemanding. If you are giving a plant to a forgetful waterer, select a gift tolerant of neglect. A kalanchoe will forgive not being watered right on schedule; the fussy poinsettia will wilt miserably as soon as it becomes dry. The longevity of these living gifts depends on making the right choice. It is not the only factor, of course, but the blooming period of Christmas plants is short enough without hastening its end unnecessarily.

Wrapping Christmas Plants

Plants purchased on a cold day from a reputable nursery, florist shop, or garden center are often wrapped in a paper, foil, or cellophane sleeve for protection against the elements. Though Christmas plants flourish in a cool home, they can be severely damaged by even brief exposure to below-freezing temperatures. I once witnessed the irretrievable demise of a lovely poinsettia in the 45 minutes it took me to drive home from a garden center. The courtesy of a protective sleeve is not usually provided at a drugstore or supermarket, so you may want to think twice before buying a plant from these places when the temperature is below freezing.

A plant that is purchased, wrapped, and taken home as a gift for later presentation should be unwrapped until you are ready to give it away. It takes only a few days for a poinsettia left inside a paper sleeve to lose its lower leaves, or for a Christmas cactus to drop unopened flower buds. Plants can be rewrapped easily on the day of delivery.

To wrap a plant, gently lay the plant on its side on top of a piece of paper large enough to surround the plant. Simply roll the paper around the plant, making a cone, and tape the paper to the sides of the pot. Then stand the plant upright and neatly fold and staple the top of the paper cone.

Although florists usually use a sleeve of plain brown paper to protect plants, a self-styled model can be made of Christmas wrapping paper or colored foil. Both are ideal for gift-giving and festive when decorated with colorful ribbons or bows. When giving a foil-wrapped plant, you might suggest that the recipient remove the foil completely instead of pulling it down around the pot. I would give the same advice for plants purchased in foil-wrapped pots. A container sitting in foil cannot drain properly when watered. At the least, you should poke drainage holes through the bottom of the foil. Also, decorative colored foil sometimes competes harshly with the flower colors and can actually detract from a plant's appearance.

POINSETTIA

Yuletide Symbol

Scientific Name: *Euphorbia pulcherrima*
Origin: Mexico

In 1828, while serving as the first U.S. minister to Mexico, Joel R. Poinsett introduced to the United States a plant which has become as much a symbol of the holiday season as the Christmas tree. He was subsequently honored by having that plant, the poinsettia, named after him.

The poinsettia has become the nation's most popular plant gift. Its bright red bracts and green leaves signify the Christmas season; it is given as a decorative Yuletide house plant and used as a source of cut flowers for holiday arrangements. In warm regions of the country, including Florida and Hawaii, the poinsettia is a common flowering shrub.

Description

What most people think of as the flower petals of a poinsettia are really colored leaves called "bracts." The true flowers are the insignificant greenish "buttons" found in the center of the bracts. These unique blossoms, known as cyathia, characterize the euphorbias, a botanical group that includes not only poinsettias but also other popular garden and house plants, such as flowering spurge (*Euphorbia corollata*) and crown-of-thorns (*Euphorbia splendens*).

Up until about twenty years ago, poinsettias had the untimely habit of dropping leaves and flower bracts—often before Christmas. The poinsettias brought home by Mr. Poinsett, fabulous as they might have been, were wholly inferior to the plants available today. They were also leggy and spindly. Fortunately, in the last twenty years these Yuletide favorites have undergone dramatic improvements at the hands of plant breeders, including the development of larger flower bracts, new colors, and, most important, greatly superior keeping qualities.

Many people believe that the poor qualities of early poinsettias are properly attributed to the poinsettias of today. This is simply untrue. Shops are now filled at Christmas with the beautiful new-era poinsettia, bearing pink and cream-colored bracts as well as the traditional red. Commercially, red is the overwhelming favorite, however. These new poinsettias can hold their colorful bracts far longer—often until Easter.

Breeders continue to work on improving poinsettias and in recent years have developed varieties with shocking pink, mauve, orange, and even bi-colored bracts. One of the new novelty varieties, Jingle Bells, has bright red bracts mottled pink. Since poinsettia sales are improving annually, these new introductions will surely make it to the mass marketplace over the next few years.

It is widely believed that poinsettias are poisonous. The fact is, where plant parts have been eaten, some rare instances of local irritation (stomach pains with vomiting and diarrhea) have been documented. Since small children are often attracted to the poinsettia's bright colors, it is a good idea to keep the plant out of harm's way. In addition, poinsettias, like other euphorbias, contain a milky white sap, called latex, in both stems and leaves. When the plant is cut, the sap oozes freely and may cause a poison-ivy-like reaction or severe eye irritation on contact. You should exercise care when pruning or potting.

Availability

Since the new poinsettias last longer than the old-fashioned varieties, plants are now appearing in the marketplace as early as Thanksgiving. Retail outlets generally feature and sell the plants until Christmas, but you will be hard pressed to find a poinsettia for sale at any other time of year, particularly a good-looking one. As with other Christmas purchases, it is best to buy early before the pickings become slim.

Selection

In larger nurseries, or even supermarkets, you may have hundreds of poinsettias to choose from—at least if you get there early enough. Sometimes the demand outstrips the supply as early as mid-December. So despite the hassle of selecting the best plant from among hundreds, it is better than selecting from among sorry leftovers. To choose the best poinsettia out of a crowd, keep the following points in mind:

• Choose a plant with leaves down to the bottom of the stems. This indicates the plant has been well cared for and has an active and healthy root system.

• Pick a poinsettia with flower bracts and leaves that are fresh looking, not wrinkled, withered, curled, or yellow—all signs of a lack of water or a possible nutrient deficiency.

• Look for a plant with a few upper bracts that still show a trace of green—the plant's peak of perfection is yet to come.

• Avoid buying a plant that has exuded white latex from leaves or stems. While this may simply indicate damage from rough handling, it could be evidence of a more complex problem involving moisture availability and cell damage.

During the Holiday Season

While plant breeders deserve (and surely some have received) blue ribbons for developing vastly improved poinsettias, one original quality remains: fussiness. Without proper care, plants may not last through the season in top form, and, with today's plant prices, a week or two of glory is simply unacceptable.

LIGHT: Poinsettias are more than Christmas ornaments. They are living plants requiring ample light. To help assure a thriving plant, provide 3 to 4 hours of direct sunlight daily by placing the plant in front of a sunny window.

TEMPERATURE: Poinsettias stay freshest in a cool room. If it is too hot, lower leaves may suddenly drop, and plants will look faded and lackluster. Night temperatures of 55–65° F. and day temperatures of 65–70° F. are ideal.

MOISTURE: Water your poinsettia when the top layer of soil in the container feels clearly dry to the touch. The frequency of watering and the time it takes for the top layer to dry will depend on pot size, soil type, and environmental conditions in your home. If you rely on your sense of touch, you cannot go wrong. Always water thoroughly, until the water runs through the drainage holes in the bottom of the pot. Wait about 15 minutes and then discard any excess water that has accumulated in the drip plate beneath the container.

Warm rooms also tend to be dry. Since the poinsettia is native to a moist subtropical environment, humidity should be increased if plants are kept where temperatures exceed those recommended. If necessary, place the plant on a large saucer or tray filled with constantly moistened pebbles or pea gravel. Do not allow the water level in the tray to go above the top layer of pebbles, since plants sitting in water often suffer root damage.

FERTILIZER: Commercial growers kept your poinsettia on a regular fertilizer schedule for months before sending it to the marketplace. There is no need for you to add more nutrients until early spring.

PLACEMENT IN THE HOME: Never place the poinsettia in a draft—from a window, doorway, or heating unit. When placing plants in front of a window, take care to prevent the leaves or bracts from touching cold window panes.

Following the Holiday Season

Most people do not want to bother with the poinsettia after Christmas—and for good reason. Its care is time-consuming, and forcing it to bloom for the following Christmas can be tricky. If you think your time would be better spent on other gardening tasks, do not feel guilty. Keep and care for your plant until the bracts have dropped and then, with a free conscience, throw it out or give it to a friend who might be more inclined to deal with it.

On the other hand, if you cannot bear to discard a living plant and feel you must at least try to carry your poinsettia over for next Christmas, the following paragraphs will help you achieve success. A properly tended plant becomes larger and more beautiful each year, so successfully bringing one into bloom for a second time is rewarding. Proper care should assure the life and health of your plant for many years to come.

LIGHT, TEMPERATURE, MOISTURE, AND FERTILIZER: After the bracts have dropped off, continue to provide the poinsettia with at least 4 hours of direct sunlight each day by keeping it directly in front of a bright window. Just pretend it is another house plant—even though less attractive than most. Cool temperatures, 55–65° F. at night and 65–70° F. during the day, should be maintained. Naturally, in summer your home will be a bit warmer— that is expected and perfectly acceptable. Continue to water the plant thoroughly when the top layer of soil feels dry to the touch. Provide a pebble tray if temperatures are much higher than suggested. The tray is a far more effective way to raise humidity in a dry room than misting plants with an atomizer—a messy and often forgotten task.

When the plant begins to make new growth, likely in early spring, begin applying a water-soluble chemical fertilizer as directed on the package label. A product with a composition of 15–30–15 is ideal. There are several products available that will fill the bill, and all are suitable as long as the directions are carefully followed. Remember: With fertilizer, more is *not* better; too much may cause severe damage.

POTTING AND SOIL: Poinsettias, like other plants, will eventually require repotting. Your plant is ready for a larger container if you see roots growing through the drainage holes in the bottom of the pot, or when the soil dries unusually fast between waterings. Sometimes water runs through the soil more quickly than in the past, indicating the soil mass is filled with roots and a larger container is needed. If your plant has been growing ac- tively, you can bet there has been a compensating amount of root growth, and a new pot is required. Plants grown in tight containers produce smaller leaves, drop leaves despite proper watering, and just lack *oomph.*

Select a new container which is 1–1½ inches larger in diameter than the old one. A plant that is jumped from a 4-inch pot to a 7-inch pot often suffers because the overabundance of soil around the roots tends to stay wet too long and root rot may result. Most poinsettias are sold in plastic pots and should be repotted into plastic. If the initial container is clay, stick with clay so the finicky poinsettia will not have to make any more adjustments than necessary.

A suitable growing medium consists of equal parts of packaged potting soil and perlite. Perlite, a type of volcanic ash used to improve soil drainage, is widely sold in plant shops and garden centers, as well as supermarkets and drugstores.

PRUNING: Plants should be pruned after the flower bracts have begun to drop. Prune stems to a height of 6–8 inches without worrying whether any leaves remain. In a few weeks new growth will commence. This may seem drastic, but it is guaranteed to result in a far superior specimen in the long run. For some reason, many people cannot bear to give a plant a hard pruning—a phobia well worth overcoming in the case of poinsettias. Without pruning, your plant is apt to become an overgrown, bare-legged, gawky specimen, bearing little resemblance to the one you purchased or received as a gift. All pruning cuts should be made cleanly just above a node, the point where a leaf is attached to the stem. After pruning, return the plant to its sunny windowsill and continue to water and fertilize as recommended.

Propagation

This is the payoff—a showy grouping of poinsettias for the price of one. What could be more satisfying than a fabulous display produced from last year's leftovers? The tips of healthy, vigorous side shoots that have not produced flower bracts make the best cuttings. The cuttings should be 3–4 inches long. As always, the cuts should be made just above a node, the area where roots form most easily.

The simplest way to root poinsettia cuttings is to put them in a glass of water. This is often not recommended because roots that form in water are inferior to those that have grown in a solid medium such as vermiculite. Yet, when stuck in vermiculite, poinsettia cuttings often wilt and die before any roots have formed. This happens because the plant leaves lose water to the atmosphere through a process known as transpiration, and in the beginning there are no roots to take up moisture in compensation for what is lost. So I advise most home gardeners to use the glass-of-water method. Placing the cuttings in water keeps them turgid during the rooting process, increasing the chances of success. Before placing the cuttings in water, let the cut stems dry until they stop oozing the milky sap.

A small drinking glass is ideal for rooting cuttings. Cover the top of the glass with aluminum foil poked with holes to keep the cuttings in place. Change the water often so it stays fresh. The cuttings should be exposed to indirect sunlight and kept in a warm spot, not less than 70° F.

Once the roots on the newly taken cuttings have grown to about 2 inches, pot each cutting separately in a 3-inch plastic container filled with the soil-perlite medium. Cover the newly potted cuttings with a large jar or plastic tent for a few days. Then gradually adjust the new plants to the environment by opening the plastic or removing the jar for increasingly longer periods each day—2 hours, 4 hours, 6 hours, and so on. Once the young plants can survive life on the outside without wilting, place them on a sunny windowsill or in a similar environment, along with the mother plant, and provide them with the same care.

Future Christmases

After the danger of frost has passed, the poinsettia should be placed outside in a spot that gets the morning sun but is sheltered from the hot afternoon rays. (Check with your local Cooperative Extension Service for the latest recorded frost date in your area.) Bury the pot in the ground up to its rim so the roots will stay cooler and the plant will not blow over in the wind or rain. If you live in an apartment and cannot move the plant outside, leave it on its sunny windowsill and continue to care for it as if it were outside. During summer, pinch back the growing tips every few weeks to produce a bushy multi-flowered plant for the next Christmas season. Continue to fertilize as recommended on the label of the product used. Plants placed outdoors will require frequent watering—every day if the weather is warm and dry. Check daily to see if your plant needs watering by poking your finger into the soil.

If all goes well, by autumn you will have a large, well-branched specimen with several growing tips, each with the potential to bear colored bracts. Before the danger of the season's first frost, or by October 1, whichever comes first, bring your plant back inside. It is likely that it will need repotting at this time.

Once indoors, the poinsettia should be subjected to 14 hours of total uninterrupted darkness and given as much direct sunlight as possible in between. Obviously, the best time for the dark period includes the night hours, and, even so, finding a spot that is totally dark for 14 hours may present a problem. Obvious choices are a closet, spare room, or cellar. But if the closet is frequently opened at night in search of a hat or coat, if laundry is done in the cellar after nightfall, or if the spare-room door is left ajar admitting light from the hallway, such areas must be disqualified. Nor does a living-room or family-room windowsill fill the bill, since reading lamps and television sets turned on in the evening cast light which interrupts the dark period, thereby preventing flower formation.

In the event that an appropriate spot does not exist in your home, the plant can be placed each evening inside a black, plastic trash bag tied at the top. To prevent the plastic from touching the foliage, you can fashion hoops from wire coat hangers and anchor the ends in the soil. The hoops will hold the plastic above the leaves. Whether the poinsettia is kept in a spare room during the forcing period or placed inside a trash bag, you

65

should continue to water thoroughly when the top layer of soil feels dry to the touch.

The fact that many dedicated gardeners fail to produce a blooming plant by Christmas can usually be attributed to one of three causes. First, the night temperature recommended for poinsettias is between 55° F. and 65° F. Closets, spare rooms, and the inside of a plastic bag tend to be too warm and stuffy. This causes leaf drop and may prevent flowering. So a cool room, whether or not the plant is inside a plastic bag, or a closet that backs onto an outside wall is essential. Second, total uninterrupted darkness is difficult to provide, and this crucial requirement often goes unfulfilled. Third, removing the plant from the dark each morning is an easily forgotten task. Abundant sunshine during the day is as important as total darkness at night.

Believe it or not, persistence has its reward. After you have moved the poinsettia from the dark to light and back again each day throughout the fall, color will begin to show in the bracts. At this point the shuttle is over, and the plant can be cared for in a cool, well-lit spot to adorn your home for another Christmas holiday and repay you for your efforts.

RIEGER BEGONIA

The Latest Rage

Scientific Name: *Begonia* hybrids
Origin: Hybrid

The long-blooming Rieger begonias (pronounced Rye-ger) are Christmas show stoppers. Their many varieties differ in color and flower form, but all have one common trait: a blooming period that can last for months. These floral masterpieces were developed in Germany by breeder Otto Rieger and introduced to America by an Ohio nursery which supplies propagating stock to commercial growers.

While visiting a very busy garden center just before Christmas last year, I noticed a whole stand of Riegers among the multitude of poinsettias, kalanchoes, and Christmas cacti. What a refreshing addition they made to the more standard fare. Though at present Riegers are not as widely known or grown, or as popular as most of the other winter bloomers, it is almost certain that they will soon take their place among the more traditional holiday offerings and become a major part of the Christmas plant scene.

Description

During the winter months, Rieger begonias produce a profusion of gorgeous blossoms in various shades of red, white, pink, yellow, rose, and orange. Some varieties have four-petaled flowers called "singles." These flowers look like the blossoms of a wax begonia but are larger and flashier. Other varieties produce multi-petaled blossoms called "doubles," which are reminiscent of small camellia flowers or rose blossoms. If properly tended, both types will bloom over a period of several months.

Because there are enough different types of begonias to boggle the mind, plus countless hybrids of each type, people often ask where Riegers fit into the scheme of things. To simplify the classification of begonias, plant scientists divide this massive group into four categories based on the stem or root structures. The four begonia categories are: fibrous-rooted, rhizomatous, tuberous, and bulbous.

Fibrous-rooted means nothing more than a mass of threadlike roots, like those found on most other plants. The most well-known members of the fibrous-rooted group are the wax begonias (*Begonia sempeflorens*), widely grown, summer-blooming annuals used for bedding and borders. The rhizomatous group grows from a rhizome, a thick, stem-like structure which may be erect or may creep along the soil surface. Rhizomatous begonias include the rex begonias, prized for their sensationally colored and patterned leaves. The tuberous begonias grow from a bulb-like structure called a tuber, which looks like a thick piece of stem. Tuberous begonias are among the flashiest members of the family and in my opinion the hardest to grow. They include many of the large-flowered, hanging-basket types widely sold in garden centers and through mail order companies. The bulbous group, those growing from an underground bulb-like formation, originally included a single species, known botanically as *Begonia socotrana*—named after its homeland, Socotra. It was this species that Otto Rieger crossed with other species to produce the Riegers.

Availability

Riegers flower during the whole of winter and are sold throughout the blooming season. They are plentiful at both Christmas and Easter, but scarce at other times of the year. Riegers are prized for their flowers; as foliage plants, they don't really cut the mustard. So retailers, unlikely to find ready sales off-season, do not generally carry them out of bloom.

All types of businesses are cashing in on the soaring popularity of house plants—supermarkets, drugstores, and street vendors are all getting into the act. However, at present, Riegers are not widely marketed, and to find one you may have to go to the local florist shops or specialty stores. You can rest assured, though, that any extra effort spent in locating a fine specimen is worth the trouble.

Selection

The toughest thing about selection, once you have found a source of Riegers, is choosing among them. When it comes to color and flower type, one hybrid is more glorious and alluring than the next. Even the most decisive shopper can spend a good deal of time picking a Rieger begonia. But do not choose on the basis of color or the number of flower petals alone. You also want a healthy plant. Here are a few tips.

• Begonias are prone to several foliage fungus diseases which cause yellow or brown spots and blotches on the leaves. Avoid buying a plant that shows any signs of trouble.

• Choose a stocky, well-branched specimen, not one that is leggy or spindly, indications that the plant was grown where temperatures were too high or light intensity too low.

• Though the flashiest plant in the shop will have all the flowers fully opened, the best buy is the one with plenty of buds in all stages of development. You want the plant at its peak of color in your home, not in the store.

During the Holiday Season

Riegers, like all begonias, have exacting requirements for care. The closer you can meet these requirements, the longer the blooming period will be—up to 4 months and sometimes longer. If your home is a little warm or dark, enjoy the plant for as long as the flowers last and forget about carrying it over, since this can be a tricky and frustrating business.

LIGHT: During the flowering period, plants should be provided with bright indirect light. Too much light at this time may cause the flowers to fade early. Too little light may cause plants to stretch toward the light source and cease blooming earlier than they should.

TEMPERATURE: The Riegers not only prefer, but *require*, low night temperatures to stay in flower and retain their stocky growth habit. Night temperatures in the 50° F. range and day temperatures around 70° F. are excellent. A cool room or indoor porch is ideal. A plant grown where it is too warm will soon become a gawky mess bearing little resemblance to the showpiece you acquired.

MOISTURE: Newly acquired plants should be watered when the top layer of soil feels dry to the touch. Always water thoroughly, until water runs through the drainage holes in the bottom of the container. Then wait about 15 minutes and discard any excess water that has accumulated in the drip plate beneath the pot. Be careful not to overwater, a common cause of begonia fatalities. Too much water causes tubers, rhizomes, bulbs, and roots to rot. Constantly wet soil also creates a perfect breeding ground for fungi, to which the begonias are particularly susceptible. When watering Riegers, and for that matter all begonias, avoid splashing water on the foliage. Wet leaves are more prone to disease than dry ones.

Begonias grow best where humidity is between 40 and 60 percent. Since most homes are not this humid, especially during the winter months, place plants on a pebble tray as you would poinsettias (page 62). The leaves of begonias grown in a dry room become crisp around the edges.

FERTILIZER: Blooming plants should be fertilized monthly with a water-soluble chemical fertilizer recommended for use on house plants. A product with an analysis of 15–30–15 is ideal. Be sure to follow the package directions carefully.

PLACEMENT IN THE HOME: Any area which meets the requirements for temperature and light is fine and sure to be enhanced by the addition of a Rieger begonia. My only advice is to avoid drafts, either hot or cold, and do not allow the leaves to touch cold window panes.

Following the Holiday Season

After the long blooming period for Riegers, many people are tempted to throw them away, particularly when they learn that carrying them over is time consuming and chancy. If conditions inside your home are appropriate, I recommend an attempt.

LIGHT, TEMPERATURE, MOISTURE, AND FERTILIZER: Continue to provide bright indirect light. Night temperatures in the 50° F. range and day temperatures around 70° F. should be maintained. Keep fertilizing every month. Water as before, when the top layer of soil in the container feels dry to the touch.

When all flowers have faded and there are no buds left on the plant, which for well-tended specimens may be up to 6 months after purchase, it is time for your Rieger to take a rest. Allow the soil to dry completely for 10 days. Then water only when the top *half* of the soil in the pot feels completely dry to the touch.

POTTING AND SOIL: An ideal growing medium consists of equal parts of packaged potting soil, perlite, and vermiculite. When repotting Riegers, always set the old root ball ½ inch or so higher than the new soil line to assure good drainage and avoid root and stem rot. It is time to repot Riegers after you have pruned the plants as described in the following paragraph. As always, repot into a container that is only 1–1½ inches larger in diameter than the old pot. This is particularly important with begonias, which do poorly when overpotted.

PRUNING: After the 10-day dry period, prune the stems to 3 inches in height. It is sometimes painful to cut a once-glorious Rieger down to mere stubs, but it is the only way to force new growth from the bottom of the plant. The next crop of flowers will form on this new growth. Use a sharp knife or shears to assure a clean, unjagged cut. After pruning, remove any dead or diseased leaves from the soil surface and from the bottom of the plant.

A few times during the growing period that follows the rest, pinch off the stem tips, making all cuts just above a node, the place where a leaf joins the stem. This will encourage branching and promote a bushy habit.

Propagation

As with other hybrid plants, seeds collected from Riegers will not breed true. This means that the plants grown from these seeds will not usually be like the parent from which they were collected. Therefore, Riegers are propagated by stem cuttings, which can be rooted in a clear plastic box, as described for kalanchoes (page 87). (Most Riegers are patented plants and cannot be legally propagated for sale or distribution without permission of the patent holder.)

Future Holiday Seasons

Continue to water plants only when the top half of soil in the container feels dry to the touch, until new growth appears. Then begin watering when just the top *layer* of soil feels dry.

Once plants have begun growing again, place them in front of a sunny window where they will receive 4 hours of direct sunlight each day. It is essential at this time that night temperatures be in the mid-50's and day temperatures be not higher than 70° F. Plants grown where it is too warm will be leggy, not stocky or bushy. Begin fertilizing every 2 weeks with the same water-soluble chemical fertilizer you were using before.

Plants should flower again in several months, though exactly how long this will take depends on growing conditions in your home. If you succeed, you have something to be proud of.

CYCLAMEN

Dazzling Holiday Sensation

Scientific Name: *Cyclamen persicum*
Origin: Middle East

Cyclamen is the crown jewel of Christmas offerings. This plant has everything: large exquisite flowers that contrast dramatically with truly handsome patterned leaves, plus a blooming period of several months. But beauty has its price. Cyclamen is often the most expensive plant available during the Christmas season.

Plant prices generally depend on the cost of production, and it can take twice as long to produce a saleable cyclamen as required to grow a marketable poinsettia or kalanchoe. Not only do cyclamen tie up growers' greenhouse space longer, they also require more specialized care than most other holiday plants. This adds up. Nonetheless, the cyclamen's outstanding beauty and long blooming period make the extra cost easier to swallow. They are my personal favorites for the holiday season.

Fortunately, in recent years, horticulturists have developed what they call a fast-crop cyclamen program. In essence, they have figured out a way to grow large-sized cyclamen in half the time. This new scheduling breakthrough, now being put into practice by several commercial growers, promises savings at the garden center and increased popularity in years to come.

Description

People compare cyclamen flowers to butterflies, birds in flight, falling stars, and other ethereal natural wonders. They are available in white and shades of pink, red, and lavender. There are also some varieties with frilled edges to their petals, but I have rarely seen them offered for sale. Cyclamen blossoms rise on long stalks above heart-shaped leaves that are exquisitely decorated with silvery or light green markings. If plants are properly tended, the flowers open in succession from December through April.

Cyclamen grow from a fleshy red root, known to plant scientists as a corm. The corm is similar in appearance to a beet. When the cyclamen is on display, the corm is usually hidden beneath the foliage, and many people do not realize it is there until repotting time. Gardeners are frequently surprised to learn that such uncommon beauty grows from such a strange-looking root.

Cyclamen come in two sizes and, consequently, two price ranges. The large and most showy varieties reach a height and width of about 12 inches. The "mini" forms attain half that size and are ideal when space and funds are limited. Both are available in the full range of colors, both are tended to exactly the same way, and both make delightful gifts.

Availability

Cyclamen lovers anxiously pursue this plant during the Christmas season, for that is when it's most easily found. It is not unusual, though, to find cyclamen in the shops from December until Valentine's Day—another perfect holiday to present someone special with this beauty. Occasionally, you see cyclamen offered before December, but you should avoid buying one of the early birds. It is likely to have been overforced by an anxious grower in a rush to get it to market, and plants grown too quickly may not survive average home conditions as well as the later arrivals will.

Selection

Selecting a cyclamen is a simple matter. Just pick the plant with the greatest number of flower buds. After all, you pay top dollar and want to be assured the longest possible blooming period. The buds are hidden down in the center of the plant, so you will have to move a few leaves around to check it out. What you should find are buds in various stages of development—some almost tall enough to poke through the foliage, others just hovering above the corm. Do not worry about the number of fully opened flowers; those will come later. My only other advice is to pick a healthy, robust plant in the color you like and the size you can afford. As always, be on the lookout for anything crawling and keep a special eye out for the presence of cyclamen mites, described on page 153. As the name implies, this pest is particularly fond of cyclamen.

During the Holiday Season

When you see how super the cyclamen looks in your home, wherever placed, you will be willing to pull out all the stops to keep the plant and its bloom healthy for as long as possible. Cool temperatures are the key. The higher the temperature, the shorter the time a cyclamen will stay in top shape.

LIGHT: Provide the cyclamen with as much light as possible by placing it in front of the sunniest window in your home. Many people worry unnecessarily about foliage burn on plants kept too close to a window. There really is no such thing as too much light between late autumn and early spring.

TEMPERATURE: Cyclamen prefer lower temperatures than any other plant described so far in Part 3. Night temperatures in the 40–50° F. range and day temperatures less than 68° F. are perfect. You will probably have to place the plant in the coldest room you have—perhaps an inside porch or chilly entranceway will fill the bill. If your home is too warm, the cyclamen will survive for a period of time and should certainly last through the holiday season; however, the blooming period may be cut very short, and the foliage will yellow earlier than normal.

MOISTURE: Many gardeners recommend watering the cyclamen daily. I disagree. If the soil is kept consistently too wet, the corm may rot. Of course, if the soil becomes too dry, the flower buds may die before maturing. I find that what works best is watering when the top layer of soil in the container feels dry to the touch. Always water thoroughly, until water runs through the drainage holes in the bottom of the container. Then wait about 15 minutes and discard the excess water that has accumulated in the drip plate beneath the pot.

It is often recommended that the cyclamen be watered from below by pouring water into the saucer beneath the pot, waiting until the top layer of soil feels moist, and then discarding the excess water left in the saucer. Proponents of bottom-watering claim that the corm is apt to rot when water is poured into the center of the plant, accumulating in the depression on top of the corm. Watering from below can be time consuming and a pain in the neck. You will do just as well to water from above by pouring water just inside the rim of the pot, not into the center of the foliage. This method is easier and poses absolutely no threat to the corm.

FERTILIZER: Fertilize plants every 2 weeks with a water-soluble chemical fertilizer recommended for use on indoor plants. A product with an analysis of 15–30–15 is ideal. As always, follow the package directions carefully.

PLACEMENT IN THE HOME: It is unlikely that the coolest room in your home is where you want to show off the cyclamen at its peak of color. It is perfectly acceptable to move the plant into the living room while entertaining or use it as a centerpiece on the dining room table. Just remember to return it to the cool growing area before going to sleep at night, and insure as much light as possible at other times.

Following the Holiday Season

The attachment that many people form to the beautiful cyclamen causes them to go to great lengths in maintaining the plant and carrying it over. Make no mistake: It is not an easy task. However, follow-up telephone calls from those who try it at appropriate temperatures disclose a fairly high success rate. I recommend taking a chance.

LIGHT, TEMPERATURE, MOISTURE, AND FERTILIZER: Continue to provide as much light as possible. Keep night temperatures between the 40's and low 50's; day temperatures should be less than 68° F. In summer it may not be possible to keep the growing area this cool—just place the plant in a spot that's well ventilated. Fertilize every 2 weeks as before.

Throughout the blooming period continue to water when the top layer of soil begins to feel dry. In March or April the plant will stop blooming, and the leaves will begin to yellow. The cyclamen will enter a dormant state, and the corm will undergo a ripening process, an essential part of its growth cycle. At this point, you should only water enough to keep the soil from completely drying out and the corm from shrivelling. As a result of this dry treatment, all the foliage will turn completely brown and will eventually fall from the corm, a process which may take up to 2 months. Do not pull the leaves off prematurely, because a piece of the corm may also be pulled off, leaving it vulnerable to disease infection.

By the time the cyclamen is totally without foliage, it will be about May or June. At this time, you can move the plant to a less obtrusive spot until new growth begins, which should be by the end of summer. Many people place the potted cyclamen corm outdoors for the summer, claiming the new growth is sturdier and plants fare better than those left inside.

POTTING AND SOIL: After all the leaves have fallen and before placing the plant outside, repot the corm into a container that is 1 inch larger in diameter than the old pot. Cyclamen that are overpotted tend to bloom less freely than those in tight containers. The top half of the corm should be placed above the soil line; the bottom half should be below ground. This will help assure adequate drainage and avoid corm rot caused by moisture accumulation. Also, a corm allowed to sit half in and half out of the soil seems, for some reason, to produce a more floriferous plant.

A soil mixture of 2 parts packaged potting soil, 1 part peat moss, and 1 part perlite is ideal. It is rich enough to support a healthy plant, and it drains well.

PRUNING: Cyclamen are not generally pruned or shaped. The only growth that is removed are leaves that have yellowed or turned brown. Leaves should not be pulled off. Instead, cut them off at the bottom, a bit above the corm, or wait for them to drop naturally.

Propagation

Commercial growers raise cyclamen from seed, but this is a tricky business that is rather difficult to duplicate at home. I would settle for carrying over the same plant, a challenge all its own. With proper care, your cyclamen will grow larger and lovelier each year.

Future Holiday Seasons

During summer, check regularly to see if the plants need watering, and continue to water only enough to keep the soil from completely drying out and the corm from shrivelling. There is no need to fertilize until new growth begins.

When you see new leaves emerging from the corm, which will probably occur at the end of summer, move the plant back to the spot where you originally had it and provide the same care as described with regard to light, temperature, moisture, and fertilizer. There is no need to provide short days as with poinsettias and kalanchoes in order to get the plants to bloom.

Whether or not the cyclamen will flower by Christmas depends on the specific environmental conditions in your home. You cannot count on a plant in full bloom for the big day. But getting a cyclamen to bloom a second time is one of the indoor gardener's greatest challenges, and, if you succeed, congratulate yourself on a tricky job well done.

JERUSALEM CHERRY & ORNAMENTAL PEPPER

Fruiting Favorites

Scientific Name: *Solanum pseudocapsicum*
Origin: South America

Scientific Name: *Capsicum frutescens*
Origin: South America

Unlike other Christmas plants, Jerusalem cherry (*Solanum pseudocapsicum*) and ornamental pepper (*Capsicum frutescens*) are not prized for their flowers. Their value stems from the spectacular fruits with which they abound during autumn and which remain through the holiday season. Both are members of an economically important plant family known to botanists as the solanaceae, a group that also includes potatoes, tomatoes, eggplant, and tobacco. Jerusalem cherry and ornamental pepper have similar cultural requirements, and both are gaining in popularity as Christmas gifts.

The fruits of ornamental pepper are an edible type of chili pepper. They are, however, extremely hot and have surprised more than one indoor gardener. The peppers are usually oblong, although their shape varies depending on variety. The fruit generally starts out green, turns white, then yellow, then purple, and finally red or bright orange. Frequently all the colors appear on the plant simultaneously.

The fruits of Jerusalem cherry are not real cherries and are not edible. Keep this plant away from children who are apt to be attracted to the colorful fruit. The fruit of Jerusalem cherry is round, usually about the size of a marble, and is bright orange or yellow—both colors appear concurrently.

Availability

Jerusalem cherry and ornamental pepper are most commonly found during autumn. Their fall colors make them naturals as Thanksgiving gifts or as part of decorative Christmas arrangements. Since both are easy to care for, relatively inexpensive, and plentiful, they are quite irresistible.

Selection

The most important thing to look for when selecting either a Jerusalem cherry or an ornamental pepper is fruit in various stages of development. You want to be sure of getting as much mileage as possible from the plant you purchase. Also, check carefully for the presence of whiteflies, described on page 155. Look for them on the undersides of leaves, where they normally feed. Both plants are particularly prone to this nuisance, and you do not want to risk infesting your entire indoor plant collection by bringing home a pest-ridden plant.

Cultural Requirements

The Jerusalem cherry requires night temperatures of 50–55° F.; the ornamental pepper grows best where it is warmer at night, 60–65° F. Day temperatures of about 70° F. are perfect for both. When deciding which of these novelties to give as a gift, consider temperatures in the recipient's home.

Both plants require about 4 hours of direct sunlight daily and should be placed in front of a bright window; both should be watered when the top layer of soil feels dry to the touch; and both should be fertilized monthly with a balanced water-soluble chemical fertilizer recommended for use on house plants.

Properly tended plants stay in fruit about 6 weeks, though it is not uncommon to obtain 8 to 10 weeks' worth of color from them. Inevitably, however, the fruits will dry and drop off, and the leaves will be shed. At this point, the growth cycle has ended and plants should be discarded.

Both the Jerusalem cherry and ornamental pepper are treated as annuals; that is, they last for one season only. They are grown commercially from seed and produce insignificant white flowers which are followed in autumn by the fruit. At the end of the fruiting period, in late winter or early spring, plants irretrievably decline in vigor.

People sometimes become very agitated when told that it is time to toss out a cherished plant, even after it has lost all its fruit and the leaves are falling like rain. But growing the Jerusalem cherry and the ornamental pepper is like growing annual garden flowers that bloom in summer and are killed by the first hard autumn frost. The only difference is that the colorful season for these fruiting beauties is fall, and the cycle ends in winter. When you think of it that way, discarding the plant does not seem so tragic.

Knowing that both of these plants are perennial in their native lands tempts some people to try and carry them over by giving plants a hard pruning after the fruit has fallen in the hopes of encouraging new growth from the base. What usually results are disgraceful-looking specimens not worthy of display. I do not recommend trying to rejuvenate these old plants. It just does not seem worth the effort.

Propagation

The seeds of Jerusalem cherry are sown between January and March; those of ornamental pepper are sown in early spring. The method of starting seeds described for kalanchoes (page 87) works well for both of these plants. Seedlings that have produced two sets of leaves should be potted individually in 3-inch containers filled with a mix of equal parts of packaged potting soil and perlite. The young plants can be brought outdoors during summer. A spot that gets the morning sun but is protected from the hot afternoon rays is ideal. I would leave the 3-inch pots in some type of flat or shallow box where they cannot be blown over in the wind or rain.

While plants are outdoors, check daily to see if watering is needed. Soil in small pots tends to dry very quickly, and it may be necessary to water every day when temperatures are high. Also, during this time, pinch back the growing tips every few weeks to encourage branching. Repot when needed, using the recommended mix. Bring plants back indoors before the first frost. If you live in an apartment, provide the seedlings with direct morning light and protection from the afternoon sun during summer, and care for as described.

By early autumn you should have flowers from which fruit will develop, as well as small green fruit soon to change color. Care for them as recommended with regard to light, temperature, and moisture. You should have a full display of color for late autumn.

Seeds of Jerusalem cherry and ornamental pepper can be purchased through the mail order companies listed in the appendix. There are several varieties well worth trying, many of which are not ordinarily seen in the shops, which may make you want to grow them all the more.

HOLLY

Christmas Foliage

Scientific Name: *Ilex* species
Origin: Widespread

Exchanging gifts of holly is a common tradition of the Yuletide season. Bright red berries set against lustrous dark green leaves reflect the holiday color scheme and conjure images of Christmases past. While live holly plants in containers are now appearing in the shops during the season and are sure to gain in popularity as gift plants, cut branches still lead the way for holiday decoration and gift giving. Cut holly branches are a charming way to say "Merry Christmas," whether you buy them from a garden center or a Christmas tree lot, or snip them from plants in your own backyard.

Cut Holly

The two species of cut holly most often used for Christmas decoration are English holly (*Ilex aquifolium*) and American holly (*Ilex opaca*). There are hundreds of varieties of each, which vary in leaf size, shape, and color; habit of growth; and fruit characteristics. Cultivated varieties of each are grown in commercial orchards strictly for use at Christmas, the way Christmas trees are raised. The cut holly industry, centered in the Pacific Northwest, is very big business.

Imaginative plant lovers have created a multitude of attractive ways to display cut holly branches—in mixed arrangements, as mantle ornaments and centerpieces, on doors, in wreaths, and so on. Its many uses fit into two general categories: dry or in water.

Dry branches may be used to decorate stairways or mantles, or may be placed around an arrangement of winter fruits, or small tips may simply be taped behind a door knocker. The beauty of dry branches is short lived; they may not last longer than a few days. As the foliage dries, the berries darken, shrivel, and soon drop. So it is best not to start too early if you plan to decorate for a special occasion with dry holly branches.

You will get far more mileage out of holly branches if they are kept in water. Used this way, there is almost no limit to the arrangements that can include or feature holly. Branches cut when temperatures are above freezing may last up to a month indoors.

Have no fear if the branches cannot be placed in water right away.

They will survive a journey to a friend's house as long as the ends are re-cut before you place them in water. Make the cuts at an angle so there is a larger surface to take up moisture. Re-cutting the branches just before they go in water assures greater longevity. Other tips to insure the freshest-looking holly for the longest time include: washing the cut branches in warm soapy water, then rinsing well in cold water; removing any yellow, brown, or damaged leaves; removing any foliage that will be submerged in water (underwater leaves rot easily, causing stems to become clogged and preventing them from taking up sufficient moisture); and changing the water every few days to keep it algae-free.

Living Plants

Garden centers now carry small living holly plants prepackaged for holiday gift giving. Live holly plants in containers are lovely in the home during the holidays but should not stay indoors for more than a week. Holly is not a house plant, and the warm dry air in our homes will do them in if they are left inside too long. During their brief indoor stay they should be misted with water daily to keep the leaves from drying. The soil should be kept evenly moist but not soggy.

Holly must be planted in the ground outdoors soon after it has been acquired. It will not do to leave the plants above ground in their containers outdoors where temperatures are low. Anything less than 20° F. will cause severe and probably irreparable root damage. Obviously, if the ground is frozen, you will not be able to plant the holly and may lose it by the time the ground is ready. Therefore, if you live in a northern climate, a live holly plant is not a suitable gift. You had better stick with the more traditional holiday plants or cut holly branches.

In warmer areas, where holly can be planted outside during the Christmas season, the gift is a more suitable one. Evergreen holly is a wonderful addition to gardens that lie within its hardiness-zone range. This plant is not only handsome the year-round but is also relatively undemanding.

Hollies do well in partial shade where the soil drains easily. The soil should be slightly acid, so mix some peat moss into the topsoil at planting time. Newly planted shrubs should be watered thoroughly to help settle the soil around the roots and get plants off to a good start. A layer of mulch should be applied to retain soil moisture essential to young plants. Shrubs should be tended carefully the first year by watering during dry periods between spring and late autumn.

Before planting, be sure to find out which species or hybrid of holly you have acquired and how large it ultimately grows. Many types grow into large trees over 45 feet tall. You want to provide adequate space for future growth to assure your holly a long and healthy life.

NORFOLK ISLAND PINE

Tropical Christmas Tree

Scientific Name: *Araucaria heterophylla*
Origin: Norfolk Islands

Though Christmas plants usually bring to mind such flowering favorites as poinsettia and kalanchoe, there is one plant associated with the season which is grown strictly for its foliage. It is the Norfolk Island pine (*Araucaria heterophylla*). A beautiful shape and perfect symmetry make this plant among the most beloved subjects for the indoor garden at any season, a favored living Christmas tree and a popular Yuletide gift.

The Norfolk Island pine bears tiers of graceful branches densely clothed in needles, ½ inch long. Well-grown plants are a beautiful dark green and are very nice to touch. During my days at the U.S. Botanic Garden I often noticed that people were fascinated by the large specimens of Norfolk Island pine on display and invariably reached out to touch them.

This plant is native to the Norfolk Island, a tiny island in the South Pacific, where it reaches a height of 200 feet. It is hardy in the warmest parts of the United States, including southern Florida, where gorgeous specimens abound.

Availability and Selection

The Norfolk Island pine is raised by the boat load in commercial greenhouses specializing in foliage plants. They are available during the holiday season in sizes ranging from 6 inches to 6 feet, and priced accordingly. You will not have trouble finding a specimen at any time of year in the plant stores, though the selection may be a bit more limited away from the holiday season.

Whether you buy a large specimen for use as a Christmas tree and later as a floor specimen, or a tiny plant for the windowsill garden, you should choose carefully. Look for plants with healthy branches down to the soil line. Poorly grown plants react first by dropping lower branches. Also, you should be able to gently shake the plant without it shedding needles, another indication of cultural malpractice. A well-grown plant will be comparatively stocky; that is, the spaces between branches will not be long. Of course, this point is relative, and you should see lots of Norfolk Island pines before you decide on this criterion. My only other advice is to select a plant that is dark green, not yellow or faded looking.

Cultural Requirements

The Norfolk Island pine should be given as much direct light as possible from mid-autumn through spring. During summer protect it from the hot afternoon sun by closing sheer curtains, partially closing Venetian blinds, or moving the plant back a few feet from a bright window. To keep the plant growing symmetrically, give it a quarter turn every week to prevent it from bending toward the light. Night temperatures of 50–65° F. and day temperatures of 68–72° F. are ideal.

When the top layer of soil feels very dry to the touch, water thoroughly until water runs through the drainage holes in the bottom of the pot. Wait 15 minutes and then discard any excess water that has accumulated in the drip plate beneath the container. The Norfolk Island pine is frequently overwatered, so be sure to feel the soil before watering. The biggest complaint about the Norfolk Island pine is that it drops lower branches or needles. A common cause of this problem is a lack of humidity. This can be corrected with the use of a pebble tray as described for poinsettias (page 62). Fertilize the Norfolk Island pine every 6 weeks with a water-soluble chemical fertilizer recommended for use on foliage house plants, and follow the package directions carefully.

When it is time to repot, select a container that is 1–1½ inches larger in diameter than the old one. A medium of equal parts of packaged potting soil and perlite is recommended, with a tablespoon of bone meal or other slow-release fertilizer mixed into the bottom half of the mix.

Propagation

Norfolk Island pines are commercially propagated by seed. Though tip cuttings will take root quite easily, cutting off a piece of the plant permanently destroys its symmetry and natural form. If you desire a whole family of Norfolk Island pines, you would do best to purchase small specimens and grow them, or purchase seeds, which are available from mail order companies (see the appendix).

KALANCHOE

A Bright Surprise Among the Succulents

Scientific Name: *Kalanchoe blossfeldiana*
Origin: Madagascar

The kalanchoe is the most mispronounced house plant in the land. The proper pronunciation of this increasingly popular flowering beauty is ka-lan-KO-e. It rolls off the tongue in a pleasant melodic way.

The kalanchoe is a member of the Crassula family, a widely grown group of succulents represented in most indoor gardens by the ever-popular jade plant and in most outdoor displays by the echeverias, commonly known as hen-and-chicks.

Description

Kalanchoes bear a canopy of garnet red, orange, yellow, or salmon flowers above a dome of thick, waxy green leaves. The richly colored flowers give the plant an umbrella-like appearance from afar. Close up, you can see the hundreds of star-like blossoms comprising the canopy. There are spectacular tall-growing varieties which reach about 1 foot in height, as well as mini forms about half that size.

Like other succulents, kalanchoes store water in their leaves and stems, the way cacti do, though not in the same quantity. For this reason, kalanchoes are reasonably drought resistant. If you have selected this plant for the forgetful waterer on your shopping list, you have made a wise choice.

Availability

The kalanchoe is another of the short-day plants. It blooms naturally when nights are long and days are short, making winter its general time of availability. Commercial growers, however, cleverly trick the plants into bloom for any season by hanging black cloth over the plants for 14 hours each day. The black-cloth trick is performed for variable periods of time depending on the date flowers are sought. Though seen in shops most often during the Christmas season, kalanchoes may also be found in full bloom for Valentine's Day and during the autumn holidays. In fact, you could probably find a specimen at almost any time, though it might not be in flower.

Selection

Selecting the right kalanchoe means beautiful blossoms for several weeks and a lovely winter windowsill display. To be sure of getting the best possible buy, keep certain points in mind while shopping.

• Choose a plant with most of the flowers still unopened, not one in full bloom. The peak is yet to come.

• Select a specimen that is compact, not one with long spaces between the leaves. A leggy plant may have been grown under higher than recommended temperatures or lower than optimum light levels.

• Pick a kalanchoe with plump fleshy leaves. Wrinkled or puckered foliage indicates improper watering, and you may never get the plant to look quite right.

During the Holiday Season

With a minimum of care, the many tiny flowers of kalanchoe will open in succession, providing a lasting show for the holiday season. It is important, though, to provide the little attention the plant requires so it will remain a healthy specimen worthy of carrying over for Christmases to come.

LIGHT: The kalanchoe, like other succulents, requires abundant sunshine to retain its compact growth habit. Plants provided with lower than adequate light levels become leggy as they reach for what little light is available. You should provide a minimum of 4 hours of direct light each day by placing the plant in front of a sunny window.

TEMPERATURE: Like most winter bloomers, kalanchoes grow best where it is cool. Night temperatures of 50–60° F. and day temperatures of 65–70° F. will help assure the longest possible blooming period and promote a stocky growth habit.

MOISTURE: Water the kalanchoe when the top half of the soil in the container feels dry to the touch. The frequency with which this occurs depends on several factors, so you must rely on your sense of touch, not the calendar, to tell you when it is time to break out the watering can. As with other pot plants, always water thoroughly until water runs through the drainage holes in the bottom of the container. Remember, the kalanchoe is a succulent, a member of one of nature's most resourceful plant groups. To carry itself through dry periods, this plant stores water in its leaves and stems. Overwatering causes stem rot at the soil line—the cause of death among more succulents than you can imagine. If your kalanchoe turns yellow, it is likely to be overwatered. At that point the plant is probably irretrievable.

FERTILIZER: If plants are purchased in bloom, there is no need to fertilize until the flowering period is over and new growth has begun. Otherwise, fertilize with a product recommended for flowering house plants as soon as you see new leaves developing. Be sure to follow package directions carefully. Plants that are not growing do not need to be fertilized.

PLACEMENT IN THE HOME: Everyone wants to show off a plant that is in full flower, and nothing adorns the coffee table or mantle like a kalanchoe blooming its head off in December or January. In the evening or anytime after you have provided its 4 hours a day of direct sunlight, feel free to move the plant wherever you like—just return it to the window the next morning.

Following the Holiday Season

The foliage of the kalanchoe is quite attractive. The dark green waxy leaves have scalloped edges, making the plant as attractive and interesting as many house plants even without the drama of flowers. Meeting the following cultural requirements will enable you to maintain a healthy, good-looking plant between flowering periods.

LIGHT, TEMPERATURE, MOISTURE, AND FERTILIZER: Continue to provide a minimum of 4 hours of direct sunlight each day, just as you would for any other succulent. Cool temperatures should still be maintained in order to keep plants sturdy and compact. Continue to water thoroughly when the top half of soil in the pot feels dry.

When you see new growth, it is time to begin fertilizing. Any of the fertilizers labeled for use on flowering house plants is suitable as long as the directions are carefully followed with regard to frequency of application and amount.

POTTING AND SOIL: Kalanchoes are usually repotted after flowering. Select a container 1 – 1½ inches larger in diameter than the old one. For example, a plant growing in a 4-inch pot would be placed in a 5–5½-inch container. A soil mix of equal parts of packaged potting soil and sand works well. Do not use fine sand or beach sand, but a coarse grade of builder's sand— the type with little bits of gravel scattered throughout.

PRUNING: After plants have flowered, cut back each stem below the flower stalk and just above a node, the point where a leaf joins the stem. During the active growing period, usually between early spring and late summer, pinch back each growing tip by cutting off a pair or two of leaves. This encourages branching and produces a full specimen with a multitude of growing tips, each capable of bearing a tuft of blossoms. Use sharp shears to assure a clean, unjagged cut.

Propagation by Cuttings

Kalanchoes can be propagated by cutting the stem tips and inserting them in vermiculite, a mica-like material available in garden shops and plant stores. This can be done anytime except when plants are in bloom. Cuttings should be removed just above a node, as if you were pruning the plant. Pinch the lowest pair of leaves off the new cutting and allow the cut end to dry for several hours, a practice followed in the propagation of all succulent plants. You can simply lay the cuttings on a paper towel to dry.

An easy way to provide the humidity needed for cuttings to root without wilting requires filling a clear plastic shoe or sweater storage box halfway to the top with vermiculite. Pour enough water over the vermiculite to make it evenly moist but not soggy. Insert the dried cuttings deep enough to anchor them firmly, but do not allow the lower leaves to touch the vermiculite, or they may rot.

Make a few air holes in the lid of the box with a hot nail and put the lid in place. Keep the container in a cool room out of direct sunlight so the temperature inside does not get too high. In a few weeks the cuttings will root.

When there is a small mass of 1–2-inch roots, pot the plants individually in 3-inch containers or plant a small group in a larger pot, using the soil-sand mixture. (Don't worry if you pull a cutting out before it's ready, just carefully replace it and check again in a week or so.) Once the newly potted cuttings begin growing, pinch them back every few weeks to encourage branching, and tend to them as you would the mother plant.

Propagation by Seeds

Purists say the best home-grown kalanchoes are started from seed, since they adjust from the outset to the environment in which they will grow. Seeds of the latest and greatest varieties are available from several of the major mail order plant companies. If you are adventurous, give it a try. Although there are as many opinions on the best way to grow plants from seeds as there are gardeners, the method I recommend requires a minimum of equipment and works as well as any other system I have used. Milled sphagnum moss, a commonly sold horticultural product available in plant shops, is an excellent medium for germinating seeds.

- Start with a 5–6-inch, clay bulb pan. These are the shallow clay pots sometimes called azalea pans.
- Fill the bottom third of the clay bulb pan with clay shards. You can make your own by breaking up an old clay pot.
- Thoroughly soak the needed amount of sphagnum moss in a bowl of water. The only way to be sure of getting the moss well moistened is to dunk it entirely in the bowl and then squeeze it like a sponge to get rid of the excess moisture.
- Fill the bulb pan with the sphagnum moss up to about ½ inch from the top.
- Place the seeds evenly over the top of the moss, about 2 inches apart. Then cover the seeds with dry sphagnum moss applied in a very thin layer; it should be just sprinkled on to a depth approximately equivalent to the thickness of the seed. If the seed is ⅛ inch thick, that's how thick the layer of sphagnum should be.
- Immerse the bottom half of the pot in a pan of water until moisture is visible on the top. Remove the pot from the water pan.
- Cover the top of the pot with plastic wrap in which you have punched a few small air holes with a toothpick or pencil point. The plastic will keep the moss moist, which is essential to prevent the seeds from drying out, a common cause of failure in getting seeds to sprout.
- Check regularly. When the top layer of moss begins to feel dry to the touch, water from below as just described. Never water from above, or the seeds may become dislodged and be carried down through the moss. Avoid overwatering, a cause of damping off, a disease that rots newly planted seeds before they sprout or rots newly sprouted seeds at the soil line.
- Keep the container in bright but indirect light and provide night temperatures of 55–60° F. and day temperatures about 10 degrees higher. A spot in front of a north-facing window or several feet from a sunny exposure would be fine.
- Once the seeds have sprouted and developed two sets of leaves, gently prick the seedlings out of the moss and pot them individually in tiny 1½-inch "thumb" pots, or 3-inch pots if the smaller size is unavailable.
- Provide the newly potted seedlings with high humidity for at least a week by keeping the pots in some sort of terrarium or under a large jar propped up just enough to allow some air movement inside.
- Gradually adjust the young plants to the world outside the terrarium or jar by placing them with the mother plant or in a similar environment for increasing periods of time each day—2 hours, 4 hours, and so on.
- Begin caring for the young plants as you would the mother plant.

Future Holiday Seasons

Though kalanchoes are short-day plants, blooming in their native lands when nights are long, they usually flower under average indoor conditions during spring. For Christmas flowering they must be subjected to 14 hours of total uninterrupted darkness daily, with as much light as possible in between, from September 1 to early October. Providing a dark period as described in the poinsettia section (page 65) is imperative. But keep in mind that the number of weeks that the dark period is necessary is shorter for kalanchoes than for poinsettias.

If you do not wish to subject your plant to the rigamarole of short days and shuttles to and from windowsills and closets, and are satisfied with a spring-blooming kalanchoe, just tend the plant as described and let nature take its course.

CHRISTMAS CACTUS

A Long-Time Favorite

Scientific Name: *Schlumbergera bridgesii*
Origin: Brazil

The Christmas cactus is one of nature's most beguiling achievements. Satiny-petaled flowers dangling from the tips of oddly segmented stems make this plant one of the season's best gifts. The Christmas cactus is also quite fascinating botanically. It is a member of one of the plant kingdom's most unusual groups, the epiphytes.

Epiphytes are plants that grow on other plants, usually referred to as hosts. In their native habitat, Christmas cacti are generally hosted by trees growing in the tropical rainforest and are found on parts of the tree that receive ample light. They are held firmly to the host by strong roots. Most orchids and bromeliads are also epiphytes. Although epiphytes thrive on the host plant, they are not parasites, since they derive no sustenance from their host. Rather, they are nourished by organic debris which collects and decomposes around their root systems.

Description

The Christmas cactus is a multi-stemmed plant; each of the dark green stems is segmented at 1–2-inch intervals. Tiered flowers are born on the ends of the stems, giving the plant a graceful, arching appearance. Christmas cacti are available in a wide range of colors including lilac, deep rose, salmon, red-orange, and white. Often the blossoms are bi-colored, normally a combination of white and a pastel. All the varieties are lovely.

Many people consider the name Christmas cactus to be a misnomer and are surprised to learn that this plant is, in fact, a cactus. Confusion stems from the plant's general appearance, so different in form from the barrel-shaped or spine-covered plants familiar as stereotypical cacti. But botanists classify plants by flower structure, not by general appearance, and the flowers of the Christmas cactus are structurally similar to those of their desert-dwelling relatives. Of course, there are major differences, since the Christmas cactus is native to the Brazilian tropics, where it grows high in the trees of the rainforests, not rooted in the desert sands.

Classification of this plant is not the only source of confusion. The Christmas cactus is very similar in appearance to its cousins, the Easter cactus (*Schlumbergera gaertneri*) and the Thanksgiving or crab cactus (*Schlum-*

bergera truncata, also known as *Zygocactus truncatus*). However, each blooms at a different season as denoted by its name. All three are frequently referred to as Christmas cacti since few people can distinguish among them. Here is how to tell one from the other:

• The stem segments of the Christmas cactus have scalloped margins. Blooms are generally found at the stem tips only.

• The Easter cactus is more likely to bloom between the stem segments, as well as at the stem tips.

• The Thanksgiving or crab cactus has two to four pointy teeth along the margins of the stem segments. Blooms are generally found at the stem tips.

Availability

Acquisition of the Christmas cactus is quite easy. Any plant shop that carries seasonal plants is sure to sell Christmas cacti in bud or bloom during the holiday season. Shops specializing in house plants may also sell them at other seasons, though they may not be in flower. I recommend buying a Christmas cactus off season. It is likely to cost less, and bringing it into bloom for Christmas is quite manageable.

Selection

Healthy specimens are generally abundant during the holiday season. Therefore, the toughest thing about buying a Christmas cactus is deciding which color to choose. Once you have made up your mind as to color, there are just a couple of pointers to keep in mind.

• Pick a Christmas cactus bearing large, ready-to-open buds. They are more likely to stay on the plant. Tiny buds seem to drop off between store and home in rebellion to the change of environment.

• Choose a plant with firm stems that are a rich, green color, not puckered, curled, yellow, or brown—all indications of a moisture problem, either too much or not enough.

During the Holiday Season

Christmas cacti are not fussy plants. Unless their environment is changed while small buds are developing, you are likely to be successful in maintaining the delicate blooms.

LIGHT: Plants purchased in bud or bloom should be exposed to bright indirect sunlight during the flowering period; too much sun will cause flowers to fade before their time. "Bright indirect light" is a vague and often misunderstood term. I have always found success by interpreting it to mean placement directly in front of an unobstructed northern window; in front of a window facing east, west, or south, as long as translucent curtains are kept closed or Venetian blinds are partially drawn during the sunniest hours of the day; or at a window facing east, west, or south, where strong light is obstructed by a neighboring building or trees outside the window.

TEMPERATURE: One way of encouraging a Christmas cactus to bloom is by exposing it to low night temperatures during autumn—as close to 55° F. as you can stand. During the blooming period, and at other times, night temperatures of 60–65° F. and day temperatures about 70° F. are ideal.

MOISTURE: It has been my experience that almost all problems with the Christmas cactus can be traced to improper watering. This is no surprise since most of the guidance I have seen on watering Christmas cacti is misleading and confusing. It seems that people either forget this plant is a succulent and water it too often, or they treat it like any other cactus and don't water it enough. While the plant is a cactus and requires less water than most tropical house plants, gardeners must keep in mind that its native habitat is one quite different from that of most cacti.

Despite repeated instructions to the contrary, my Christmas cacti are watered the same way year-round, and I have always been pleased with my success. Water thoroughly when the top *half* of soil in the pot feels very dry to the touch. As always, discard the excess water that accumulates in the drip plate beneath the container about 15 minutes after watering.

FERTILIZER: The Christmas cactus grows most actively from early spring through the summer. This is the time to fertilize. Apply any of the products recommended for use on flowering house plants, following the directions on the package label to the letter. There is no need to fertilize during the flowering period.

PLACEMENT IN THE HOME: When the Christmas cactus is in bud, especially during the state when buds are showing color but are still fairly small, leave the plant where it is. Moving it at this time to show it off is a common cause of bud drop, the subject of countless Christmas cactus complaints. Once the flowers are opened, you can move it for a few days, in accord with your image of where it looks best, then back to bright indirect light.

Following the Holiday Season

Once the flowers have dropped, the Christmas cactus loses its drama and is less interesting in form than many other cacti. Its real value is the ease of carrying it over for next year's show.

LIGHT, TEMPERATURE, MOISTURE, AND FERTILIZER: Most sources suggest the Christmas cactus be exposed year-round to bright indirect or curtain-filtered sunlight. This is great while plants are in bloom, since more light at this time may cause flowers to fade. However, the showcase specimens, the ones that really thrive, are exposed to higher light intensities for most of the year. I place my plants in front of the sunniest window in the house at all times except during summer and when they are flowering. In summer, when the sun's rays are really strong, I give them bright indirect light. Too much light during the dead of summer causes the stems to become flaccid, faded, and scorched.

From Christmas until autumn continue to provide 60–70° F. night temperatures and day temperatures of 70° F. Water when the top half of soil in the container feels dry to the touch. Begin fertilizing when plants are actively growing, from spring through autumn.

POTTING AND SOIL: Christmas cacti seem to grow best in clay pots. My preference likely stems from the fact that soil dries faster in clay pots than in plastic. In its native habitat, the Christmas cactus grows on trees, where water can drain freely from the root system. If you tend to be a heavy-handed waterer, pay the little extra for a clay pot; it may save you the cost of the plant in the long run.

When necessary, repot into a container that is 1–1½ inches larger in diameter than the old pot. The mix should be 2 parts packaged potting soil and 1 part vermiculite or a coarse grade of builder's sand well speckled with gravel. As with poinsettias and kalanchoes, it is time to repot when you see roots growing through the drainage holes in the bottom of the container, when water runs through the soil faster than it did in the past, when the soil dries more quickly than usual, and when there has been a lot of new growth since the last repotting. I wouldn't hesitate to move a Christmas cactus from a plastic to a clay container, a practice cautioned against with many other plants.

PRUNING: After it has flowered, prune the Christmas cactus by cutting off a few of the "links" or sections from each stem tip. You can pinch them off with a fingernail or a pair of scissors to assure a clean cut. Pruning encourages branching and the production of more stem tips, each having the potential to bear a flower. So if you are after a large plant loaded with flowers, this task should not go undone.

Propagation

Once you see how easy it is to propagate the Christmas cactus, you may end up with enough plants to supply everyone on your shopping list. Plants can be propagated at any time of year, except after they have set bud or are in bloom. Simply remove 3–5 segments from the stem tips and insert the cut ends in moist vermiculite. Roots form easily. The plastic storage box method described for rooting kalanchoes (page 87) works

93

beautifully for the Christmas cactus and assures that the plants will root before wilting.

Once cuttings have developed a mass of 1–2-inch roots, pot them individually in 3-inch pots, or plant small groups in a larger container using the recommended soil mix. Tend to their light, moisture, temperature, and fertilizer requirements as described for the mother plant.

Future Holiday Seasons

It is well known that the Christmas cactus is another of the short-day plants, blooming when nights are long. However, most people do not realize that it will flower if night temperatures are low, regardless of day length. Providing night temperatures of 50–55° F. from early November until the plants set bud is all it takes. The average indoor temperatures during the day are just fine.

Plants kept on the windowsill may automatically be exposed to low night temperatures. I give my plants no special treatment, just leave them on the cool kitchen windowsill during autumn. Every year without fail, they are filled with flowers during the Christmas season. The portion of the plant closest to the window sets buds first, since it is exposed to lower temperatures than the inside half. At that point, I turn the plant around, and buds eventually set all over. This results in a succession of opening buds and an extended blooming period. This method does not guarantee plants at their peak of color by Christmas morning; they are off by as much as three weeks before or after the big day. I don't know if you could time them any more accurately, but for such a minimum of effort, who can complain?

If you don't have a cool window, all is not lost. You can still force plants into bloom if night temperatures are in the 55–70° F. range, by subjecting them to 14 hours of total uninterrupted darkness from the middle of October until buds set. Instructions for providing a dark period are included in the discussion on poinsettias (page 65).

PART 4

Year-Round Offerings

Happy Birthday, Happy Anniversary, Welcome Home, Happy House Warming, Get Well Soon, I'm Sorry, I Love You, Congratulations

Exchanging gifts to mark special events or to say something personal is an ordinary and recognized occurrence in our society, and plants offer a wide range of gift choices. The selection may vary, but the perfect plant can be found at any time of year to mark a special event or to say anything you want to anyone.

The list is just endless. The events celebrated by everyone in the nation, such as birthdays, anniversaries, Mother's Day, Father's Day, and Thanksgiving are only the tip of the iceberg. You can provide a living symbol at any time to show how important a particular event really is or how you feel at that moment. Accompanied by a floral gift, sentiments like congratulations, thank you, cheer up, or get well soon take on special significance. Years ago, upon the dissolution of a relationship with a boyfriend, I received a single long-stemmed red rose with a note saying "Je regrette." No doubt this gesture was lifted from a Grade B Hollywood movie, but corny and trite as it was, I'm still talking about it.

Many plants are so commonly identified with a particular event they seem to speak for themselves. Others need a little help. A cactus accompanied by a card that says "I love you" gets the message across despite the unlikely association between love and cacti. A cactus in flower, a real treat, needs no accompanying words.

The chart on page 97 contains a brief list of occasions that provide the opportunity to present a plant. Each suggested gift reflects my subjective judgement of the appropriate plant as well as information on general availability at that time of year. You will likely have even better ideas.

Matching Friends with Flowers

I must admit that in the past I would not have thought of presenting my husband with a dozen roses or an orchid plant, but it occurs to me now that he would probably be thrilled.

Give your friend, lover, relative, acquaintance, spouse, boss, or whomever, the plant gift you think appropriate for the occasion. Satisfaction is guaranteed, and anything goes. Don't overlook the opportunity to give roses or orchids, for example, just because the recipient is a man.

You should, however, keep in mind the horticultural habits of the recipient and the cultural requirements of the plant. The concept of a living gift encompasses renewable pleasure lasting far beyond the event or reason prompting the gift. The more demanding gardenias and orchids are best left to devoted gardeners. A carefree pothos or aglaonema, both to be described, suits the more casual gardener. Cacti are for friends with a sunny windowsill, while the African violet will perform marvelously under a fluorescent light fixture in the total absence of natural light.

Sources

Local plant stores, garden centers, and florist shops offer a wide variety of plants ideal for giving throughout the year. The selection will depend on the market in your area; shops in more populated locations generally carry a wider variety of plants. However, for many of the plants described in this section the selection offered by mail order from specialty nurseries surpasses the quality and quantities available anywhere else.

There are companies specializing in African violets that offer hundreds of varieties representing different colors, leaf types, and flower forms. Many of these African violet specialists offer the increasingly popular miniature and trailing violets, frequently hard to come by in the shops. It is doubtful that shops in your town carry more than a few different orchid plants, but there are several commercial growers who mail order more species and hybrids than you probably thought existed. The widest variety of cacti and other succulents is available through mail order growers (see the appendix). They sell plants representing dozens of different genera, many of which are just as easy to grow as their more common cousins but less likely to be found in local markets.

My experience in ordering plants for the U.S. Botanic Garden has shown that most specialty nurseries are small, family-operated businesses that take great pride in their offerings and provide the utmost care in wrapping and shipping plants to their customers. Though not all nurseries grow the high-quality plant material we consumers should demand, most are highly reputable and a pleasure to deal with.

OCCASIONS AND EVENTS TO REMEMBER

Occasion	Appropriate Gift Plant
New Year's Day	A member of the aroid clan, such as a philodendron (page 136), pothos (page 136), or spathiphyllum (page 138). All three should last through the new year and will generously provide additional gifts. For more show, try one of the plants described in Part 3.
Valentine's Day	An African violet (page 99) in full bloom. Few plants are easier to come by, more reasonably priced, or more welcomed.
Saint Patrick's Day	What could be more appropriate than a rich green foliage plant to mark this day (see Foliage Plants, page 135).
Mother's Day	Mom will adore a gardenia (page 106). The cost may be high, but this plant is a show-stopper.
Father's Day	An orchid plant (page 111) for the man who has everything. Some of the most enthusiastic and talented orchid growers are men. The orchids described in this section are as easy to care for as plain old house plants.
Independence Day	Why not a red-flowered anthurium (page 118) or a striking aphelandra (page 121) to mark the nation's birthday? Neither will soon be forgotten, and both are easier to grow than their exotic appearances suggest.
Thanksgiving	Chrysanthemums, of course (page 37).
Christmas	Choose any of the plants discussed in Part 3.

Half the fun of mail ordering is leafing through the catalogs. Generally, the catalogs are reasonably priced, filled with plant descriptions and cultural information, and, in many instances, provide illustrations of the plants offered for sale. Often the cost of the catalog is subtracted from the price of the plants purchased. Or you may find yourself a lifetime recipient of a fascinating publication.

I have provided a brief list of specialty growers in the appendix. While the list is by no means complete, it provides a good starting point for folks interested in ordering by mail. For obvious reasons, many nurseries do not ship plants during the cold winter months.

Wrapping Plant Gifts

Variations in climate and the distance to be travelled, as well as the shape and delicacy of your gift, bear directly on proper wrapping and transport. Once you have purchased it, protecting your gift should be your first priority, and you are better off over-protecting a living specimen, at least in cold climes. Even when the elements are not particularly threatening, you can do no harm wrapping a gardenia, cactus, African violet, or foliage plant as you would a poinsettia to be exchanged at Christmas (see page 58). Ribbons, bows, foil, and wrapping paper are as lovely a complement to plant gifts as they are to other presents, a custom entirely independent of the season. Some general thoughts on transporting the plants in this section may be helpful.

• African violets are horizontal in habit and need a full complement of leaves to remain perfectly symmetrical. Lowering an African violet into a paper cone may cause the normally brittle leaf stalks to snap. However, if the plant has not been watered for a few days, the leaf stalks become somewhat flaccid and less likely to break. Naturally, a wilted plant does not make a suitable presentation, but if you wrap when it is just about to start wilting, you've got it made. When you present the African violet, suggest that the recipient water it promptly. Placing an African violet in a shoe box and securing the pot by surrounding it with crumpled tissue paper is another way to safely present this special gift.

• The flowers of a gardenia may turn brown from being handled or even touched accidentally. Unless you can assure the plant a hands-off trip to its destination, a paper sleeve would be a wise idea.

• Contrary to popular notion, orchid plants are some of the sturdiest subjects around. If the orchid is not in bloom, you will probably not need to wrap it unless temperatures are less than 45° F. However, if the plant is bearing flowers, a cone would be helpful to prevent the tragedy of accidentally knocking off a blossom.

• Anthuriums and aphelandras should definitely be given the cone treatment if temperatures are below 55° F.

• Wrapping cacti and other armored succulents can be a real headache. Obviously, the problem is the basic incompatibility of spines with wrapping, carrying, holding, and transporting in general. The spines often catch on wrapping paper and may cause the plant to dislodge from its container or stick you or the recipient. Since cacti tolerate cool temperatures, I would forego wrapping altogether and decorate the pot with a colorful bow. You could also place the plant in a box, as suggested for African violets. Forget about wrapping large cacti.

• To wrap or not to wrap foliage plants depends on the delicacy of the species you are giving. A tiny potted fern could certainly use the protection of a paper cone, but a sturdy philodendron should do just fine unwrapped if temperatures are reasonable.

AFRICAN VIOLET

Gem of the Indoor Garden

Scientific Name: *Saintpaulia* hybrids
Origin: Africa

I have given and received more African violets than any other plant. I am as likely to be accompanied to dinner at a friend's home by an African violet as I am by a bottle of wine. As popular plant gifts, violets rank with the standard holiday fare such as poinsettias and mums. Their handsome foliage, symmetrically arranged in a flattened rosette, makes the perfect backdrop for delicate blooms which poke up between the leaves to form a bouquet in the center of the plant.

Visitors to my home usually expect to see an abundance of exotic botanical delights. You see, being a horticulturist is not without its pressures. Yet my plant collection consists of a disproportionately large number of African violets scattered about—on a party dinner table, a bookcase, or a windowsill. Friends sometimes ask why I bother with such common fare. The answer is simple: Nothing else provides a more splendid display of color and grace for so many months with such a minimum of effort. If you consider African violets passé or too common for your collection, look and think again. Alone or in groups, these beauties always get a second glance and admiring comment.

Description

African violets are members of the gesneriad family, a group that includes gloxinias and episcias as well as some lesser-known but equally charming house plants such as *Aeschynanthus* and *Nematanthus*. The name African violet is actually a partial misnomer. While the parents of modern hybrids are indeed from Africa, the plants are unrelated to garden violets—and violet is only one of many colors available.

African violet hybrids are classified in many ways, including by size. Most of the specimens available for sale and found in people's homes are called standards. They are ordinarily purchased and displayed with an 8–14-inch diameter. However, I have seen standards at plant shows well over 2 feet across with leaves as symmetrical as the spokes on the wheel of an English racer. Many of the standards sold in plant shops have the potential to reach such size and perfection with less effort than people imagine.

There are also smaller African violets, known as miniatures, which do not attain a diameter of more than 6 inches and produce proportionately smaller blossoms. Plants in between the miniatures and standards are called semi-miniatures. Though the standards are most popular, many indoor gardeners make a hobby of collecting their more diminutive cousins. "Minis" are charming when planted in brandy snifters or terrariums. There are also trailing violets, which are lovely in hanging baskets, where they bloom freely and cascade gracefully over the sides of the container.

African violets are also classified and described by flower and foliage type. Flower colors include white as well as shades of purple, violet, lavender, wine, pink, and rose. The flowers may be "single," consisting of five petals—two smaller petals and three larger ones; star-shaped, consisting of five petals of about equal size; or "double," consisting of numerous petals with either frilled, ruffled, or smooth edges, depending on variety. The blossoms may be streaked or rayed with a contrasting color. They may be edged white or edged in a contrasting color. African violet leaves may be crimped or curled or have wavy margins. They may be slightly cupped. Some leaves appear almost quilted. Others have a curly edge or are more narrow than rounded. Some African violets have variegated leaves (green with cream, yellow, or white markings) or foliage that is particularly fuzzy. In short, there is a great number of African violet types to choose from.

Violets are further classified into groups known as series. A series includes varieties that a particular hybridizer claims have special and superior characteristics. All members of a particular series are developed by a single grower. Actually, a series is more for commercial promotion than to set plants apart botanically. The Optimara, Rhapsodie, and Ballet series are three examples of popular and widely available groups of floriferous, fairly carefree plants, in a wide color range. Violets are frequently, though not always, labeled with both the series and the hybrid name.

Availability

African violets are available throughout the year from most garden centers as well as from plant and florist shops. Many grocery stores also sell violets, though the plants often look a bit neglected. Shops usually carry the more common varieties and rarely offer the miniature or trailing violets. These will probably have to be ordered from the specialty houses listed in the appendix.

Selection

African violets hybridize with incredible ease. As a result, plant breeders develop and introduce into the trade countless new varieties each year, confounding both beginners and seasoned violeteurs. Many of the new introductions are really no improvement on the older varieties and are often not much different. Many shops sell plants with labels so you generally know the name of the variety you are buying. You cannot be sure, though, how the plant will perform. Will it produce innumerable suckers that must be removed to maintain the plant's symmetry? Is it disease resistant? Will it bloom freely and frequently? If you have purchased a loser or two in the past, and everyone has, do not give up. African violets are an award-winning group with less than their share of deadbeats among the multitude of available hybrids.

Choosing a plant is more difficult than finding one. The hardest thing about selection is identifying a well-grown symmetrical specimen. For me, the beauty of this plant is as much in the symmetry of its leaves as in the flowers. To be symmetrical the plant must bear a flattened rosette of leaves arranged like the spokes of a wheel. I do not purchase plants that have produced multiple crowns or offsets (plants growing from the base of the mother plant, creating a helter skelter pattern of foliage and flowers). Though most African violets will eventually produce offsets, you do not want your plant to start out this way, or its symmetry may be destroyed forever.

Aside from scouting out a single-crowned, symmetrical plant, look for a specimen with flower stalks bearing several buds—an indication of a free flowering habit. The leaves of your plant should be horizontal, not stretched upward, a sign that the plant has been grown in too little light. In addition, African violet leaves should not hug the container, an indication of exposure to lower than optimum temperatures or poor watering practices. Avoid plants with a long bare stalk at the base, a condition indicating that numerous outer leaves have died and been removed. Finally, keep an eye out for mealybugs, a pest with an affinity for African violets. After your examination of available stock, make a choice based on color as well as the flower and foliage type you find most appealing. It is sure to be a difficult choice.

Cultural Requirements

A properly grown African violet blooms several times each year in exchange for minimal care. Providing adequate cultural conditions is not that difficult, but many people seem confused about just what it is these plants require to prosper and bloom freely. The confusion arises partially from conflicting and often vague advice in many books and magazine articles. I welcome the opportunity to help clear things up and assist you in growing the best possible African violets.

LIGHT: The most beautiful and floriferous African violets I have seen have been grown under fluorescent lights. A standard-sized fixture, 4 feet long, equipped with two 40-watt tubes—one cool white and one warm white—fills the bill perfectly. The fixture and tubes can be hung in any reasonably ventilated room where night temperatures do not drop below 58° F. My fixture is hung in the corner of a cool basement. Space under a kitchen cabinet or beneath a book shelf, in the laundry room or in a spare bedroom will also do beautifully. The light should be kept on 12 hours a day. Plants should be placed 6–12 inches beneath the tubes.

Many plant stores offer special fluorescent tubes designed and marketed for plant growth. They are more expensive, to be sure, but as far as I can see do not produce superior results.

Knowing that African violets respond particularly well to life under artificial light prompts many exchanges among co-workers in offices where fluorescent lights are banked in the ceiling. If an African violet must be kept on a desk or file cabinet several feet from ceiling lights, its leaves will stretch upward and plants will fare poorly. However, if the recipient has a fluorescent desk lamp, you are in business. An African violet or two placed right under the lamp should do just fine, provided 12 hours of light is provided and other cultural requirements are accounted for.

Do not be discouraged if the person to whom you wish to give an African violet does not have a fluorescent light fixture. A window that gets the morning sun but is protected from the hot afternoon rays (which may cause foliage burn during summer) will do fine. Fluorescent light is ideal, but natural light is adequate.

TEMPERATURE: African violets grow best where night temperatures are 58–68° F. and day temperatures are 5–10 degrees higher. Most sources recommend 65° F. as the lowest acceptable temperature for violets. I disagree. The African violets in my cool basement tolerate temperatures down to 58° F. just beautifully. However, I do not recommend suddenly moving plants to a cool growing area. Instead, they should be adjusted slowly to temperatures below 65° F. Cold drafts must be avoided, a fact to which my husband will attest. He inadvertently left a door open this past winter, and I lost the two African violets closest to the door (and my heart).

MOISTURE: African violets should be watered thoroughly when the top layer of soil feels clearly dry to the touch. Plants kept too wet may rot at the soil line; those kept too dry will wilt, lack vigor, and bloom poorly. Try not to pour water on the foliage, where it often accumulates in tiny puddles. If this accidentally occurs, simply tilt the plant slightly and shake off the water. With many fuzzy-leaved plants like African violets, water tends to cause spots on the foliage, especially on specimens placed in cooler growing areas.

African violets prefer a more humid environment than most homes afford, and plants benefit greatly from the use of a pebble tray. They also seem to do particularly well in groups, where moisture from soil surfaces evaporates after watering to humidify the air surrounding all the plants.

FERTILIZER: If you asked twenty-five African violet growers how to fertilize your plants, you would get twenty-five different answers. My plants are fertilized early every month with a water-soluble chemical fertilizer, analysis of 15–30–15, following package directions. In addition to this application I apply fish emulsion during the middle of every other month. My plants grow quickly, bloom freely, and receive rave reviews.

PLACEMENT IN THE HOME: If grown under natural light, African violets should be placed within a few feet of the window. Keep leaves from touching cold window panes and avoid drafty areas. The prettiest African violet displays I have seen are small groups arranged on glass shelves in front of a window. Glass does not overpower these delicate plants and provides an open, airy feeling.

Fluorescent light fixtures for growing African violets can be placed wherever the temperature range is suitable. When plants bloom, you can take them out from beneath the lights and move them to a coffee table or wherever they look best. Just remember to return them to the growing area within 4 or 5 days, for about a week. If plants are still in bloom and worthy of display, you can bring them out for viewing again.

POTTING AND SOIL: African violets grow better and bloom more freely in smaller pots than other plants of equal size. For example, a 4-inch pot is suitable for a plant measuring 12–16 inches across. Just keep in mind that the soil in small containers tends to dry fairly quickly, and plants require more frequent watering than those in larger pots. As long as you check regularly whether the top layer of soil feels dry, there should be no problem. I prefer the shallow plastic pots often referred to as bulb pans rather than deeper containers, because the soil in the bottom does not stay wet too long.

Plants purchased in 3-inch pots should be moved to 4-inch containers after they have made substantial growth, when the water runs through the soil more quickly, and when the soil dries more rapidly between waterings. I would not move a plant from a 4- to a 5-inch container unless it was really a show-size specimen. Overpotting is a common cause of failure with African violets.

A recommended soil mixture consists of 2 parts packaged potting soil and 1 part perlite. You can also use the packaged African violet mixes sold in many shops, but these tend to be more costly than mixing your own, and I do not think they produce superior results.

PRUNING: African violets have a natural shape and symmetry that should not be tampered with. Plants are not pruned for purposes of shaping or in an attempt to produce new growth. Leaves that yellow or turn brown can be cut off close to the stem with a pair of manicure scissors. Spent flower stalks can be removed the same way. If a flower stalk has spent blossoms in addition to unopened buds, just pick off the faded flowers with your fingernails. It is best to groom plants just before they need watering. At this point, the leaf stalks are more flaccid than usual and less likely to snap when handled, a frustrating occurrence.

Many African violet hybrids sucker freely. That is, they produce little offsets from around the base of the mother plant. As these suckers grow, they destroy the plant's natural symmetry. Check regularly for the development of suckers and cut them off with small scissors as close to the main stem as possible or gently pull them out of the soil.

Propagation

African violets are most quickly propagated by the suckers pulled off the mother plant. Every time you tidy your favorite violet, you have the opportunity to propagate new ones. Sometimes the suckers will have six or more leaves and a small root system. Often there will be no roots. Depending on the size of the suckers, you may have to remove the mother plant from the pot in order to cleanly separate the suckers.

Insert the plantlet in a clear plastic box filled with moistened vermiculite, exactly as described on page 87. Check every few weeks to see if roots have formed. Once there is a healthy mass of 2-inch roots, pot each sucker separately in a 2-inch plastic container and provide the same care as you would for any African violet.

African violets are most commonly propagated by single leaf cuttings. They should be taken from the oldest outside ring of leaves so as to play less havoc with the plant's shape. Cut the leaf off as close to the main stem as possible. Then re-cut the stalk to about 2 inches in length. Insert the leaf in a clear plastic box, as previously described. African violet leaves take weeks, possibly months, to develop a sufficient root system, trying the patience of almost anyone. The use of a rooting hormone hastens the process a bit.

Once a mass of roots has formed, pot the leaf in a 2-inch plastic container. Soon young plants will develop at the base of the mother leaf. At that time, the mother leaf can be cut off. Frequently, several young plants develop simultaneously. African violets develop two leaves opposite each other, then two more leaves, to form sort of a square. It is easy to tell when more than one plant is growing. Leave the strongest new plant in place and cut the others off at the soil line, and you're off to a symmetrical start.

SPECIAL HINTS:

• When African violet leaves rest on the rim of a clay pot, they soon wither and die. Either the pot rim cuts the leaf stalk, or the fertilizer salts that accumulate in the clay cause damage. Growers who prefer clay to plastic containers often dip the pot rim into hot paraffin, which helps prevent the problem altogether. I recommend the use of plastic pots for convenience.

• There are available in some shops and through many mail order companies gizmos called African violet rings—I love them. There are two types. One is a solid ring of plastic; the other is a ring-shaped, trellis-like affair. I prefer the latter for aesthetic reasons, but they both work well. The ring fits around the rim of the flower pot, and the outer circle of foliage rests on the ring, which holds the leaves up and out, helping to show them off and to maintain a flattened rosette. The use of these rings adds a professional touch to the display of African violets. (They will also prevent the leaves from being damaged by the rim of a clay pot.) The ring makes an ideal companion gift to the plant.

• Dust often becomes trapped between the leaf hairs of African violets. A gentle washing with plain tap water using a sink sprayer or hand atomizer helps keep the foliage clean and functioning efficiently. After washing, tilt and shake the plant so that any excess water spills off. Plants should not be placed in bright natural light until the leaves dry, or spotting may occur.

GARDENIA

The Indoor Garden's Most Heavenly Scent

Scientific Name: *Gardenia jasminoides*
Origin: China and Japan

A rich and often-imitated floral scent as well as leaves with the highest glossy shine make the gardenia a wonderful gift. However, recipients may quickly become disillusioned, for gardenias are fussy, unpredictable, and have a penchant for unpleasant problems. The gardenia is like a thoroughbred—it requires constant and doting care to perform to its full potential, but when that potential is reached, the plant has almost no equal. Judging from its long-standing popularity, I'd say my opinion is widely shared.

Description

Waxy white flowers, potentially 3 inches or more across, and a strong, sweet scent are the trademarks of the gardenia. The scent is similar to that of jasmine, hence gardenia's scientific name, *Gardenia jasminoides*. The fragrant flowers yield an oil used in fabricating perfume and scenting tea.

Gardenia blossoms may be born the year-round, though spring blooming is most prolific. While this plant is in flower, you can put away air fresheners; your room will smell like the Garden of Eden. Like the blossoms of many other white-flowered plants, gardenia petals turn brown all too soon. Generally, this has nothing to do with inept care. It is just the way of gardenias, though touching the blossoms may hasten discoloration.

The species most commonly grown indoors is *Gardenia jasminoides*. Its large-flowered varieties bear blossoms up to 5 inches across. These blossoms are used by florists as cut flowers and often make their way into corsages and onto lapels during prom season. I cannot distinguish among the gardenia varieties, and plants offered for sale are rarely labelled. Since care is identical for each, I see no great advantage in knowing exactly which form you have.

Many northerners think of the gardenia only as a house plant and envision a multi-stemmed, potted specimen 1–2 feet high, the size range of most indoor subjects. Yet in the South and on the West Coast the gardenia is grown outdoors as an evergreen shrub and reaches heights of up to 6 feet. In bloom, these shrubs are simply glorious.

Availability

Plant shops and garden centers may offer gardenias at any time of year, though they are generally more plentiful around Christmas, Valentine's Day, Easter, and Mother's Day. Plants purchased during these holidays are usually loaded with flower buds about to open. Commercial growers achieve this enticing and obviously saleable state by subjecting the plants to high temperatures around the clock to encourage rapid growth. Then they turn the thermostat down to about 60° F. at night to promote flower bud formation. In a short while plants are ready for the marketplace.

Selection

With gardenias, the season of purchase makes little difference, and whether your plant is bought with a multitude of flower buds about to burst open or just a few will soon be irrelevant. After a time the plant will adjust to conditions in your home, and with proper care it may bloom intermittently through most of the year.

When shopping for a gardenia, pay less attention to the number of buds than to general health and appearance. You want a well-branched, vigorous specimen that is pest-free. Gardenias are particularly prone to mealybugs, which I have seen cover the undersides of leaves and colonize in droves along the stems. In fact, in a relatively short period of time, infestation can become so severe that the presence of black sooty mold, a fungus disease that frequently follows insect infestation, renders the plant unidentifiable from a distance. Spider mites and soft scale insects also frequent the gardenia.

Gardenias are also prone to a fungus disease called stem cankers. Damage is frequently found at the point where the stem meets the soil line. The cankers look like sores or lesions overgrown with corky tissue which radiates from the canker. This condition causes wilting, leaf drop, yellowing, and stunted growth. Also avoid plants with discolored spots, blotches, or dead patches on the foliage, which may be caused by one of several fungi and are quite common on plants that have been grown in overcrowded areas or have been kept too wet. It is easy to see why maintaining a winning gardenia is one of the indoor gardener's most trying tasks.

Cultural Requirements

The gardenia may top the list of fussy house plants and try the patience of the most dedicated indoor gardener, but success can be achieved with proper care and a little perseverance. Few will argue that the gardenia is not worthy of the extra effort required. In bloom, this plant is stunning and has an unforgettable fragrance. In or out of bloom, the leaves shine like no others I have seen.

LIGHT: The gardenia requires at least 4 hours of direct light each day. Do not worry about too much summer sun. I have seen gardenias thrive and flower beautifully when grown in containers placed outdoors on a patio in full sun. As long as high light intensity is compensated for with ample moisture, success is yours. Maximum light is particularly important during the winter, when dull and cloudy days are the norm.

TEMPERATURE: For continuous flowering, provide night temperatures of 60° F. As mentioned, professional growers do this to force plants into bloom in time for various holiday seasons. Night temperatures above 65° F. will probably inhibit flower bud formation. Day temperatures of 68–75° F. are ideal. Of course, day temperatures will go higher during the summer, but if you water as needed, all will be well.

MOISTURE: For gardenias, the soil should be kept constantly and evenly moist but never soggy. Water thoroughly when the top layer of soil begins to feel dry to the touch. Plants kept too wet or too dry are likely to lose the lower older leaves as well as flower buds. Improper watering is a major cause of gardenia fatalities.

High humidity, a requirement too often unfulfilled, is also essential to successful gardenia care. The use of a humidifying tray is a must for all gardenias grown outside the tropics. A large saucer or watertight tray filled with pea gravel fills the bill perfectly. Pour water over the gravel, not allowing the water to rise above the bottom of the top layer of gravel. As it evaporates, the water will need frequent replenishment to humidify the air around the plant. Insufficient humidity causes bud drop, the most common complaint among gardenia owners. Misting is strictly second best for raising humidity, since it works only until the water evaporates; this occurs very rapidly when temperatures are high. Misting does, however, help keep the foliage clean and dust-free so the leaves function more efficiently.

FERTILIZER: If a plant could have an appetite, the gardenia would be ravenous. Without regular fertilization, leaves may pale, plants lack vigor, and flowering will be sparse. I suggest a granular chemical fertilizer recommended for use on acid-loving plants. The type you dilute in water and pour into the soil is ideal. Monthly applications at the full strength suggested on the label are fine, but application every other week at half strength is even better, since a more continuous source of nutrients is provided.

Gardenias frequently suffer from chlorosis, a fancy word for yellow leaves. Chlorosis is often evidenced by areas between the leaf veins turning yellow, while veined areas stay green. Chlorosis is often caused by an iron deficiency and can be easily remedied by the application of chelated iron. This product, available under several trade names, is mixed with water and poured into the soil or sprayed on the foliage, as indicated on the label. Leaves turn a darker green remarkably fast because the iron quickly becomes available to the plant. Applying iron chelate three or four times a year may help prevent chlorosis altogether.

PLACEMENT IN THE HOME: To provide ample light you will probably have to place the gardenia in front of the sunniest window in your home. Avoid drafty areas such as those near a door that is frequently opened or near a heating or air-conditioning vent. The gardenia may react to drafts by dropping leaves and flower buds.

Gardenias flourish outdoors during summer, especially in humid climates. Place them in a spot that gets the morning sun but is protected from the hot afternoon rays. They will do well in the hot afternoon sun, but the need for watering may be too great to suit your schedule. While the plant is outside, check it daily to see if watering is needed and continue to fertilize regularly. Be sure to bring your plant back inside before the danger of frost.

FLOWER BUD DROP: The most common cause of complaint among gardenia owners is flower-bud drop. It is depressing to anxiously await the opening of the lovely blossoms only to have them thwart you by dropping early. This is almost always caused by a failure to follow one of the cultural practices required, especially those of high humidity and ample light intensity.

POTTING AND SOIL: This past January I received a gardenia as a gift of congratulation on the birth of my son. It was full of buds and simply glorious. Unfortunately, the pot was covered with that unsightly red aluminum foil so commonly used by florists to make a plant look more like a gift. Upon my speedy removal of the foil wrapping, I found an even uglier commercial black plastic pot, which I could not get rid of fast enough. The gardenia deserves more than a plastic container or one that is foil wrapped. To my eye they look best in an attractive clay pot or a decorative ceramic container with drainage holes.

If you repot merely to replace an unattractive container, use a pot of about the same size. However, if your gardenia *needs* repotting— generally when roots start growing out of the drainage holes, when the soil dries out unusually fast between waterings, or when the water runs through the potting mix faster than in the past—select a new container that is 1–1½ inches larger in diameter and height than the old one. An ideal soil mix consists of 1 part packaged potting soil, 1 part perlite, and 2 parts peat moss. This mix drains beautifully, is acid enough for gardenias, and contains ample organic matter.

PRUNING: Some say that the most prolific bloomers are potted gardenias under 3 feet high and that older larger specimens bloom less faithfully. I am sure there is some truth to this theory, but an exception comes to mind immediately. There are some very large gardenias in the collection at the U.S. Botanic Garden that are over fifty years old. They are pruned back to stubs every autumn and kept in the growing houses until spring, when they are placed outside. They bloom their heads off for most of the summer. This leads me to believe that age and plant size are less important than forcing new growth, on which flowers freely develop.

In spring, before new growth commences, prune and shape plants, removing any overgrown shoots or overcrowded branches. Then snip off the ends of each stem to encourage a flush of new growth. Spindly plants that have been blooming poorly and are in need of complete rejuvenation should be pruned back to a height of 6 inches during early spring. I realize this is a painful thing for many indoor gardeners to do, but rest assured it will result in a far superior and more floriferous specimen in the long run, particularly if other cultural requirements are scrupulously met. Faded flowers should be removed promptly by cutting them off just above a node, the point where a leaf joins the stem.

To produce a few large flowers instead of many smaller ones, remove all but one flower bud from each stem. Commercial growers do this to create those splendid boutonnieres.

Propagation

Gardenias are easy to propagate from stem cuttings, which can be taken at any season. Select a 4–6-inch cutting from a non-flowering branch. Make the cut just above a node, and remove the lowest few leaves. Insert the cut end into water, and then dip into a rooting hormone, a product available in small packets from plant shops and garden centers.

Insert the cutting into a clear plastic storage box filled with moistened vermiculite, as described on page 87. In 4 to 8 weeks the cutting will root and can be planted in a 3-inch pot filled with the recommended soil mix. Provide the same care as described on page 108. Be sure to prune young gardenia plants often to encourage branching and a compact growth habit.

ORCHIDS

The Ultimate

Scientific Names: *Cattleya, Paphiopedilum,*
and *Phalaenopsis* species and hybrids
Origin: Widespread, chiefly tropical

Orchids are the ultimate plant gift. They
transform ordinary women into enchantresses,
ordinary men into exotic and handsome
strangers, and ordinary evenings into romantic
and unforgettable experiences. Give me an
orchid and I'm yours forever!

Unfortunately, many people believe that plants capable of producing
such exquisite blossoms are beyond the horticultural capabilities of amateur gardeners. While some orchids are difficult to bring into flower, indeed
even tricky to keep alive, there are beautiful orchids that make wonderful
windowsill plants and demand no more care than a gardenia. Whether pre-
sented as a plant or as a cut flower, an orchid is the superlative floral gift.

Description

The orchid family is one of the largest in the
plant kingdom, with approximately 30,000
species and countless hybrids. It is also one of
the most diverse groups in habit of growth, variety of color, flower shape
and size, fragrance, and botanical structure. There are orchid flowers that
look like insects and birds—even people. The careful study of an orchid
bloom by a group of people will surely result in a number of different opinions as to what the flower resembles.

Orchid blossoms are not only varied and beautiful, they are unique
among plants. Their sexual parts—stamens and stigmas—are fused into a
column, not separated as in most other plants. In addition, orchid pollen
is a sticky mass, not a collection of individual grains. Scientists believe
these traits are very modern in evolutionary terms, suggesting that orchids
are among the earth's newest floral masterpieces.

In nature, insect pollinators are attracted to specific orchids by special
floral characteristics, including blossom size and arrangement, scent, color
pattern, and outstanding structural features such as a pouch-like petal or
blossoms that mimic living creatures. Many orchids rely on a single species
of insect for pollination. It is easy to understand why orchids are among
the plants most intriguing to gardeners everywhere.

Three extraordinarily beautiful, popular, and widely available orchid
genera (groups of plants with similar floral characteristics) that can be
successfully grown and brought into bloom by the dedicated novice

111

are *Cattleya, Paphiopedilum,* and *Phalaenopsis.* All three are frequently recommended for beginners, yet are found in the collections of the most sophisticated hobbyists and professionals as well.

Cattleya orchids have two nicknames: corsage orchids, because their colorful blossoms are popular specimens for corsages, and bosom orchids, because that's where they often end up. "Cats," as they are called for short, are among the showiest orchid flowers. The colors are as varied as the spectrum of a rainbow. Uncommonly rich yellows, lavenders, mixtures of colors, white, and pink provide all the beauty you could ask for in a flower. There are even reds, somewhat uncommon, which are simply incomparable. *Cattleyas* have three petals. The lower petal, known as the lip or labellum, is the largest, showiest, and most colorfully marked. Set slightly behind the petals are three sepals which resemble and are colored like petals but are generally narrower. The flowers are usually 3–5 inches long, though much smaller flowered species exist, and often appear on plants about 2 feet high. Most *Cattleyas* bear one to seven blossoms one time each year. The flowering season and the fragrance depend on which variety is grown, but all flowers are long lasting unless temperatures are uncommonly high.

Like most other orchids, *Cattleyas* found in the wild are epiphytes. They grow on tree branches, usually at the edge of tropical forests. Like other epiphytes, they derive no sustenance from the plant on which they grow but take nutrition from the air and from organic debris that accumulates around their roots.

Cattleyas produce multiple vertical stems, known as pseudobulbs, which grow from a horizontal ground stem. In cultivation, the ground stem creeps along the surface of the potting medium. Flowers are formed at the leaf bases on the newest pseudobulbs. The non-flowering stems are called "backbulbs."

Paphiopedilum orchids, commonly called lady's slippers, are named for their lowermost petal, the lip, which forms a slipper-like pouch. The other two petals are narrower and frequently spotted. They may also bear hair or mole-like appendages—characteristics that only enhance their strange beauty. *Paphiopedilums,* like *Cattleyas,* have three sepals, the uppermost of which is known as the dorsal sepal. It may be larger than the other two and is usually the most beautifully colored. *Paphiopedilum* flower colors include white, green, yellow, pink, brown, and every combination of those hues. They bloom once a year, but the flowers may last for weeks, and large multi-flowered specimens may stay in bloom for months. Species vary considerably in size, though plants are usually about 1 foot high and flowers 3–5 inches.

Growing in the wild, *Paphiopedilums,* unlike *Cattleyas,* are usually terrestrial. That is, they grow rooted in the ground. The leaves are arranged in two rows, and flowers emerge singly from down in the center of the leaves. There are hundreds of hybrids, but those with mottled or spotted foliage, as opposed to solid green leaves, are easier house plants.

Phalaenopsis orchids are called moth orchids because their flowers supposedly resemble moths in flight. I must admit, though, that the moths that frequent my house do not closely resemble the exquisite and graceful flowers of *Phalaenopsis* orchids. Colors include white and shades of pink, yellow, and purple, with many striped and spotted varieties among the multitude of hybrids. Several flowers are born simultaneously on a gracefully arching flower stalk, 2–4 feet long, that emerges from the center of the plant. Moth orchids produce a handful of strap-shaped leaves, about 1 foot long. They usually bloom once a year, generally in spring, but if the flower stalk is cut back after flowers have faded, a second set of blossoms may develop. *Phalaenopsis* orchids, like *Cattleyas,* are epiphytic in their native habitats.

Availability

Orchids are available throughout the year. They are not sold in most plant shops, however; you will probably have to call the larger florist shops and garden centers to check on available stock. Even the most diversified plant businesses are unlikely to carry a wide orchid selection. However, the specialty growers listed in the appendix carry more types of *Cattleya, Paphiopedilum,* and *Phalaenopsis* orchids than you can imagine. If you have plenty of time before your gift is due, have one of the orchid nurseries send you a catalog. Then have the plant you select mailed directly from the nursery to the recipient.

Selection

Orchids are relatively expensive, although young plants may be priced under $10, especially if they have not yet flowered. Well-established blooming specimens can be very costly—I know of one rare hybrid that recently sold for $10,000. It is worthwhile to shop around and compare prices as well as stock. If you are faced with a stand filled with orchids, a rare situation indeed, here are a few tips to help in your selection.

• If affordable, buy a plant in bloom. Orchids usually bloom once a year, and if the plant is out of flower, you cannot be sure when it bloomed last or when it will bloom again. Also, I always want to see the flower color and type. There are so many spectacular varieties it seems foolish to settle for something that is not extraordinary.

• Orchids are subject to several virus diseases which cause yellow mosaic-like patterns, yellow spots, and blotches on the leaves, and a streaked, water-stained appearance to the flowers. Check the leaves and flowers carefully.

- Orchids are usually grown in a potting mixture that contains fir bark chips or tree fern fiber. The medium should look fresh and should not be broken down or decomposed—indications that the plant has needed repotting for too long.
- The newest leaves on the plant should be as large as the older leaves. If they are larger, all the better. This suggests that the current year's growth was made under proper growing conditions.
- The flowers should be firm, fresh, and waxy in appearance—not flaccid, faded, or washed out.
- Purchase orchids from a reputable dealer, preferably one that knows about orchids and can help you with a selection. The better shops may guarantee your new orchid for a reasonable period of time.
- Be sure the orchid plant you buy will suit conditions in the home of the recipient.

Cultural Requirements

Do not let the word "orchid" scare you. The only thing that is really different about orchid culture is the growing medium. Other requirements are quite similar to those described for many of the plants in this book. Of the three orchid genera I have described, the *Paphiopedilums* are the easiest to grow and happen to be my personal favorites. Their blossoms, which last for weeks, are among the most strange and beautiful flowers in the world. The *Phalaenopsis* orchids are the second easiest to maintain. Their blossoms are also long lasting. The *Cattleyas* seem to be the most difficult of the three to bring into bloom, probably because they require such high light intensity. If you can provide this crucial requirement, you will be blessed with some very flashy flowers that are sure to bowl over anyone who sees them.

LIGHT: *Paphiopedilum* and *Phalaenopsis* orchids should be placed in front of a very bright, unobstructed window. Trees growing in front of the window, drawn curtains, or nearby buildings can block out light and prevent blossoming. To prevent foliage burn during summer, close sheer curtains, partially close Venetian blinds, or move plants back from the window a few feet.

Cattleyas require more light than *Paphiopedilum* or *Phalaenopsis* orchids and grow best in front of an unobstructed south-facing window. I've been told that a good test for assuring *Cattleyas* adequate light is to determine whether there is enough light to take a photograph with an instamatic camera without a flash. If so, there is sufficient light to grow a *Cattleya* orchid.

TEMPERATURE: Despite variance in opinion as to appropriate temperature ranges, I have found, through personal experience and my observations at the U.S. Botanic Garden, that *Cattleya, Paphiopedilum,* and *Phalaenopsis* orchids will do well and flower predictably when day temperatures are 65–75° F. and there is a 5–10 degree drop in night temperature. If plants are grown near a window, they will probably experience this drop in night temperature due to loss of heat through the glass.

MOISTURE: Water orchids when the growing medium feels dry to the touch; then soak thoroughly. Since orchids are grown in a fast-draining material, you need to pour about three times as much water into the container as you would for other plants in comparably sized pots to be sure of adequately moistening the medium. With the potting materials used for orchids, you should not pour water into one part of the pot and expect capillary action to distribute the moisture throughout the medium. It will not work. You must move the spout of your watering can all over the surface of the growing medium to be sure it is soaked thoroughly. An orchid mix should not be kept constantly wet, nor should it be allowed to dry completely. Since many disease organisms thrive in a moist, dark environment, most growers water in the morning so moisture evaporates before evening. Tepid water is recommended.

Slightly reduce the frequency with which you water *Paphiopedilum* and *Phalaenopsis* orchids while they are in flower. Reduce the frequency with *Cattleyas* when new leaves have reached the size of mature leaves. Resume watering *Cattleyas* as before when new growth appears.

All three genera described here require a relative humidity of 40–60 percent, more moist than most homes. An easy way to increase humidity is to place plants on a watertight tray filled with small damp pebbles. Keep the pebbles moist by filling the tray with water up to the bottom of the top layer of pebbles. The water will evaporate from the pebbles and moisten the air surrounding the plants. Do not fill the tray to the point that the pots are sitting in water.

Syringing, or misting, plants also increases humidity, though only for a short time. Syringing is not a substitute for the pebble tray, but it can be a supplement. To help prevent disease, always syringe orchids on sunny days so that the leaves do not stay damp too long, and spray plants early in the day so moisture will evaporate by evening. Never spray plants directly at close range. Instead, spray the area around the plants so that a fine mist settles on the foliage.

FERTILIZER: Orchids growing in a mixture that includes fir bark chips should be fertilized with a water-soluble chemical fertilizer labeled 30–10–10. Apply fertilizer at the strength recommended on the label once a month—or better yet at half strength every 2 weeks for a more continuous nutrient supply. Orchids grown in a tree-fern-fiber-based mix should be fertilized with a balanced chemical fertilizer, such as a product with an analysis of 20–20–20, every month at full strength or every 2 weeks at half strength.

PLACEMENT IN THE HOME: Orchids should be placed where their cultural requirements are met. Once they bloom, you can move them to wherever they look best, as long as they are returned to the growing area after the flowers have faded. I have a large pot of *Paphiopedilums* that fills with blossoms each year. When the first flowers open, I move it from its windowsill to the living room and simply water as needed, which is far less often than when it is in the window. It blooms continuously for weeks. *Cattleya* and *Phalaenopsis* blossoms do not generally last quite as long—so they may not spend as much time in the compliment corner. Since orchids bloom only once a year, you really deserve to show them off and reap the praises.

POTTING AND SOIL: Orchids have been grown successfully in many potting materials. Consequently, the subject of growing mediums has become more confusing and frustrating than it really has to be. Most professional growers use a mix based on fir tree bark chips ("fir bark") or the fiber from the stalks of Mexican tree ferns ("tree fern fiber"). Either of these materials is mixed with a coarse grade of peat moss. You will do just fine by potting *Cattleyas* and *Phalaenopsis* orchids in 2 parts fir bark or tree fern fiber and 1 part coarse peat moss. Use the same ratio for *Paphiopedilums* but substitute a finer grade of fir bark. Tree fern fiber and fir bark chips are not easy to find. You will probably have to call shops in your area to see who carries these products, or order them from one of the orchid nurseries listed in the appendix.

It is necessary to repot orchids when the plant itself, not just the roots, starts growing over the edge of the pot. Do not repot *Cattleya* and *Phalaenopsis* orchids until you see new roots growing. If it is necessary to repot *Paphiopedilums,* wait until right after they have finished blooming.

Always repot into a container large enough to accommodate 2 years' growth. To repot, tap the plant out of its pot and remove the old growing medium from around the roots. Trim off any dead roots with a knife that you have sterilized by passing it through a flame. Clean tools help prevent the spread of virus diseases from one orchid to another. If desired, divide the plant for propagation as described on page 147.

Orchids are repotted differently from other house plants. Only *Phalaenopsis* orchids are centered in the container, because they grow up, not across. *Cattleyas* and *Paphiopedilums* grow across; they should be repotted so that the oldest part of the plant is against one side of the pot and there is ample room between it and the opposite pot wall. New growth will fill in this area.

Place broken clay shards over the drainage holes of an adequately sized clay or plastic pot. Most orchid fanciers prefer clay for its natural appearance, fast drainage, and the fact that clay "breathes"—there is an exchange of air with the outside. Fill the pot halfway to the top with one of the mixes recommended. Hold the plant over the pot so the tops of the roots are just below the pot rim. Fill in around the roots with the medium, packing it tightly. After repotting, water thoroughly. Mist plants twice daily for a week or so after potting. Orchids may require staking to stay upright.

PRUNING: Orchids are pruned to remove spent flowers and leaves that have turned yellow. Again, make all cuts with a sterile knife. After the blossoms have faded, *Phalaenopsis* flower stalks can be cut just below where the flowers developed to promote a second flowering—a special bonus with this group. The flowers of all other orchids are removed along with their stalks.

Propagation

The easiest way to propagate orchids is through division, dividing the existing plant into separate plants. Seed propagation is tricky, time consuming, and not really recommended for the beginner; it also requires special materials. However, if you are interested in growing orchids from seed, there are a number of publications on orchids that tell how to do it.

Cattleyas are divided by severing the horizontal ground stem with a sterile knife at the point where the cut will leave three or four vertical stems (pseudobulbs) per division. When dividing *Paphiopedilums* be sure there are at least two stems (leaf clusters) per division. *Phalaenopsis* orchids are divided by cutting off the top of the plant just below the point where you see roots growing from the middle. Leave the bottom part of the *Phalaenopsis* in the pot to continue growing. Newly divided orchids can be potted and cared for as described under "Cultural Requirements," page 114.

ANTHURIUM

Exotica

Scientific Name: *Anthurium* species
Origin: South America

The exotic anthuriums come to my mind at the most unexpected times, often when day-to-day pressures are getting to me. These South American natives seem to cast a spell of floral paradises, easy living, and cool tropical drinks sipped in the shade of a palm grove.

The strangely beautiful blooms of anthuriums are composed of a waxy leaf-like structure called a spathe, 3–5 inches wide and about 6 inches long, which supports a yellow column called a spadix. The spathe may be the brightest red or orange imaginable, a clear pink or white, or multi-colored. The spadix is actually made up of hundreds of tiny flowers, some male, others female—though the difference is not discernible with the naked eye. They are usually straight, but one fairly common species, *Anthurium scherzerianum,* bears a spadix curled like a pig's tail. Anthurium blooms last for weeks whether left on the plant or removed for use as cut flowers—a function for which they are becoming increasingly popular. *Anthurium andreanum,* the most commonly grown species, reaches a height of about 3 feet. *Anthurium scherzerianum* is less than 12 inches tall. Their narrow leaves are rather nondescript although not unattractive.

The anthurium is a member of the aroid family, a group that includes philodendrons, spathiphyllum, pothos, aglaonema, and monstera. Like anthuriums, all aroids produce a spathe and spadix. However, none are more dramatic than that of the anthurium.

Availability and Selection

Anthurium plants are more difficult to come by than many other flowering plant gifts, though a trip through the plant businesses in your town, via the yellow pages, should reveal a source at almost any season. Large specimens are dearly priced. For economy's sake you may wish to go with a young plant.

Large and small plants are generally sold in bloom, and I would not settle for one that does not have at least one flower bud. Look for healthy green leaves, free of any black, yellow, or brown spots, and a compact, upright specimen.

Cultural Requirements

Do not let this plant's exotic tropical appearance prevent you from buying such a unique and sure-to-be-adored gift. Anthuriums are not much harder to grow than the spathiphyllum, their close relative. They do, however, need higher humidity and more light than their cousins, requirements that are not difficult to provide.

Anthuriums require very bright indirect light. An east-facing window that gets the morning sun is perfect. A south-facing window where strong sun is obstructed by trees or neighboring buildings will also do nicely. A western exposure will suffice as long as plants are protected from the hot afternoon rays in summer; you can close sheer curtains or move plants back several feet from the window. Too much light may result in scorched foliage on the portion of the plant closest to the window. Too little light may mean an absence of flowers, spindly growth, and plants that require staking to stay upright.

Night temperatures of 60–65° F. and day temperatures of 65° F. or higher are perfect for anthuriums.

Water these plants thoroughly when the top layer of potting mix feels dry to the touch. Since anthuriums thrive in a moist, tropical environment, supply constant humidity through the use of a pebble tray.

Fertilize monthly at the full strength recommended on the label with a water-soluble chemical fertilizer high in phosphorus, such as a product with an analysis of 15–30–15. Omit fertilizer from Christmas through mid-March, while plants are not actively growing.

Grow anthuriums where their cultural requirements will be met. While they are in bloom, feel free to move these plants to the compliment corner for a week or so. When placed on a coffee table or mantle, or used as a centerpiece at dinner, the anthurium is noticeable from quite a distance. These plants are not subtle.

In nature, anthuriums grow as epiphytes on trees in tropical forests. Therefore, many growers recommend an epiphytic mix, the same one used for *Paphiopedilum* orchids—2 parts of a fine grade of fir bark plus 1 part coarse peat moss. This mix is great, but fir bark may be hard to come by. If you do not have access to this product, use a mix of 2 parts packaged potting soil and 1 part perlite.

I highly recommend clay pots for anthuriums because the soil dries more quickly between waterings, which is perfect for epiphytes. When repotting, use a container 1 inch larger in diameter than the old one.

There is a large anthurium collection at the U.S. Botanic Garden, and I cannot remember them ever being pruned. However, yellow leaves were cut off close to the stem as they appeared, and spent blossoms were promptly removed. If the plant becomes too large for the space in which it is growing, you can cut back the stem to keep it within bounds, and the plant will fare well.

Propagation

Anthuriums are easily propagated by side shoots which develop on the stems, complete with roots. This plant is almost self-propagating. The shoots can be removed below where the roots have formed and potted individually in 3-inch containers filled with the recommended mix.

APHELANDRA

Zebra Plant

Scientific Name: *Aphelandra squarrosa*
Origin: South America

The spectacular aphelandra, or zebra plant, is a regular subject of inquiry. It is also problem prone and the source of a great many complaints. Nonetheless, I see this plant often in shops, blooming its startling yellow head off, and I am certain this dramatic floral show is an almost irresistible temptation to someone in the market for an unusual gift. I have always admired well-grown specimens and find them highly worthwhile for giving.

The aphelandra is nicknamed zebra plant for its pointed oval leaves, up to 12 inches long, which are rich green and boldly striped white. Leaves are produced on stems up to 3 feet high, though most windowsill subjects are in the 1–2-foot range. Very large spikes of bright yellow flowers normally appear each fall, though I have seen plants bloom at other seasons as well.

The major problem with this plant is that it drops lower leaves no matter how well tended. Increasing humidity helps slow this irritating occurrence but does not prevent it. Eventually, you wind up with a bare-legged specimen topped with a cluster of leaves.

Availability and Selection

Aphelandras are available year-round, but you may need to do some hunting to find one. Like all plants, they are priced according to size, and the largest ones can be costly, especially when flowering. This plant even looks expensive. Buy a specimen with leaves down to the bottom of the stem. The foliage should be a rich green and clearly marked. There should be no signs of mealybugs, a regular pest of aphelandra; check the point where the leaves join the stem as well as leaf undersides for these critters. Some plants are sold with a single stem; others have been pruned and are branched. The multi-stemmed specimens seem more dramatic, though this quality may increase cost.

Cultural Requirements

There is nothing difficult about aphelandra culture, unless you count the minor nuisance of filling a pebble tray with water to keep the environment around the plant adequately humid. Otherwise, with simple care you get a lovely flower show each fall and a striking foliage display year-round.

Supply the aphelandra with very bright indirect light, exactly as described for anthuriums, page 119. Night temperatures of 60–65° F. and day temperatures 65° F. or above are ideal. Water the aphelandra thoroughly when the top layer of soil feels dry to the touch. Wait about 15 minutes and discard any excess moisture that has accumulated in the drip plate beneath the container. Check the aphelandra often to see if watering is needed. I have found that specimens grown in adequate sunlight dry out rather quickly and wilt miserably when not watered promptly. Provide a pebble tray and be sure it is properly filled at all times.

Apply a water-soluble chemical fertilizer each month as recommended on the label. A product with an analysis of 15–30–15 is ideal. These numbers are clearly marked on the package. Do not fertilize from Christmas through mid-March.

Place the aphelandra where its cultural requirements are met. Once it loses lower leaves, an inevitability you should accept at the outset, you may wish to place a smaller plant in front of it to cover the bare lower stem. A small fern or philodendron will do the job perfectly.

When necessary, repot the aphelandra in a new container about 1 inch larger in diameter than the old one. Use a clay, plastic, or ceramic container. A mix of 2 parts packaged potting soil and 1 part perlite is suitable.

Your aphelandra can be pruned by cutting back the stem or stems just above a leaf. This will force the plant to branch below where the cuts were made. Pruning results in a superior-looking specimen capable of bearing multiple flower stalks—one at each growing tip.

Propagation

When the aphelandra has grown too large and has lost its lower leaves, it can be air layered below the foliage exactly as described on page 147. This will rejuvenate your old plant beautifully. The bare stalk that remains can be left in its pot and cared for as before. Often it will produce a second crop of leaves.

Small aphelandra cuttings, 3–4 inches in length, can be taken from the growing tips in spring and rooted in moist vermiculite, either in a clear plastic box with a clear lid, or, if cuttings are too tall, under a clear plastic tent.

CACTI & OTHER SUCCULENTS

A Variety of Irresistible Forms

Scientific Name: Various
Origin: Widespread

Your search has ended if you need the perfect gift for someone who spends long summer weekends at the beach, is off on business trips whenever you call, shuttles between a city apartment and a country house, or is just plain lazy—at least insofar as caring for plants is concerned. Cacti and other succulents are ideal for friends who may not always be around to water, fertilize, prune, or repot right on time. Make no mistake: Succulents are not wholly neglectable; they are just more adaptable and less demanding of a rigorous schedule than most house plants.

Succulents are more than practical. They are plants of unusual and breathtaking beauty, with bizarre, often surrealistic, shapes and forms, exquisite leaf patterns, and gorgeous color combinations. Some people devote their entire lives to collecting succulents, each species of which is unique in appearance. They make a perfect study in textures.

All succulents, including cacti, flower predictably if cared for properly. Many produce sensational blossoms, worthy rivals to any flowers you can name. The richly colored flowers of the Christmas cactus are a good example—set against the austere and threatening-looking tentacles of the foliage, they create an artistic composition of contrast. Another example is the charming flowers of the well-known *Aloe*, or medicine plant, which resemble tiny delicate lilies and provide a dramatic contrast to the bold fleshy leaves.

Many people use the terms cactus and succulent interchangeably. This is not correct. Succulent is the more general term and refers to plants that store water. Cacti are one family of succulents—there are many other plant families that have succulent members. Therefore, all cacti are succulents but not all succulents are cacti. For example, the jade plant and the kalanchoe are succulent members of the crassula family. The *Aloes* are succulent members of the lily family. All succulents have the ability to store water for use during periods of drought, a quality which explains their relatively carefree nature. Cacti are generally leafless and store water in their stems. Other succulents store water in stems, leaves, and roots.

Trying to distinguish between cacti and other succulents can be frustrating. Both may have spines, both may be leafless, and both may have the same growth habit. However, small cushion-like structures, known as aereoles, are found only on the stems of cacti. It is from the aereoles that the spines, wool, branches, and flowers of the cactus grow.

The evolution of succulents is a fascinating study. Cacti, in particular, are one of nature's most prominent achievements. Many millions of years ago the American desert was a lush jungle. Gradually the climate changed. Rainfall decreased and deserts replaced jungles. Plants had to adapt to the changed climate, and, in order to do so, growth slowed; the leaves that lost precious water to the environment became smaller or dropped off, and the stems enlarged to store water. The stems also took over the process of synthesizing food from light, a function previously performed by the foliage. Many succulents also developed spines to protect themselves from thirsty desert animals. This ability to survive and thrive where other plants would perish makes succulents ideal plants for hit-and-miss gardeners. As you might expect, overwatering is frequently the cause of succulent fatalities, although watering every couple of months, as many people do, thinking the plants are absolutely indestructable, is equally dangerous.

Descriptions

Describing the succulents worth owning and giving would be a lifetime proposition. However, the following thirteen genera (groups of succulents) are frequently available, often asked about, and worthy of a place in any collection. There are hundreds of other succulents just as wonderful, though found less often in the shops, and their care is often identical to that required for these plants. The appendix lists several sources of the less well-known and seldom grown species as well as the more standard fare.

AGAVE (CENTURY PLANT), AGAVE FAMILY: *Agaves* are native to the Americas and the West Indies. They may be small pot plants or specimens too immense for even the largest container, depending on species and plant age. *Agaves* produce a rosette of narrow, spine-tipped leaves, usually with toothed margins. The foliage of the most frequently grown species is handsomely marked with yellow or white longitudinal stripes. Plants found in the trade are usually 6 inches to 3 feet high. Their common name, century plant, is the result of the time it takes for *Agaves* to bloom, sometimes fifty years or more. Once they do, the plants slowly die, never to bloom again. Species that flower only once and then die are known botanically as monocarpic plants. Pineapples are another example.

ALOE (MEDICINE PLANT), LILY FAMILY: These natives of Africa and Madagascar have been cultivated for centuries for their medicinal value, particularly the species *Aloe vera*. The jelly-like sap that fills the fleshy leaves is used in many countries as a soothing ointment for cuts and burns; it is also used in many cosmetic preparations. Some folks say that *Aloe* sap cures poison ivy faster than anything on the market, though I have not had such success. Nonetheless, I keep a plant in the kitchen for use on minor cuts and burns, and it works well.

Aloe leaves are arranged in a rosette. The foliage of many species is toothed along the edges and is often beautifully marked with intricate patterns that look like they were painted on with a fine brush. Delicate flowers are produced abundantly along stalks growing from the center of the plant. Many varieties sucker freely; that is, they produce plantlets at the base of the mother *Aloe*, making propagation fast and easy.

BEAUCARNIA (ELEPHANT-FOOT TREE, PONY-TAIL PALM), AGAVE FAMILY: The swollen stem base of the *Beaucarnia*, a native of Texas and Mexico, resembles an elephant's foot. The base serves as a water reservoir during dry periods. The stem tapers upward above the swollen base and is topped by a mass of hanging curly leaves, giving rise to its second nickname, pony-tail palm. In the wild, *Beaucarnias* may reach a height of 30 feet or more. Specimens under 2 feet are commonly found in the trade.

CEREUS (NIGHT-BLOOMING CEREUS), CACTUS FAMILY: Large tubular flowers of white, pink, or white and green are produced along the spine-ribbed stems of these South American natives. In the wild, plants may reach over 40 feet in height, though most specimens found in cultivation are far smaller. Most of these night-bloomers are upright-growing and free-branching. Since their flowers open at night and close by mid-morning, you may have to rise pretty early to catch the blossoms' full effect. It's worth it.

CRASSULA (JADE PLANT), CRASSULA FAMILY: There are about three hundred species of *Crassula*, mostly native to southern Africa. The overwhelming favorite and the source of more questions than any other succulent is *Crassula argentea*, the jade plant. A well-grown specimen looks like a miniature tree or bonsai and can be a truly glorious pot plant. In nature, plants may reach 10 feet high, but in cultivation, plants over 4 feet are unusual. When planted outdoors, in parts of California and Florida, they bear an abundance of pink or white blossoms. Flowering indoors is only occasional and a cause for celebration.

ECHEVERIA (ECHEVERIA), CRASSULA FAMILY: The echeverias are indigenous to Mexico and Central America. Those most commonly grown indoors produce ground-hugging rosettes of thick waxy leaves. They resemble succulent green roses and are among my favorites. In mild climates

125

echeverias are planted in rock or stone-wall gardens. Indoors they are exquisite in containers or mixed succulent arrangements. While all bear stalks of tiny flowers from the center of the plant, their most prominent features are foliage form and texture.

EUPHORBIA (CROWN-OF-THORNS, MILK-STRIPED EUPHORBIA), EUPHORBIA FAMILY: You could fill a greenhouse with *Euphorbias*—there are over fifteen hundred species native to a wide geographic area including Africa, the Canary Islands, Ceylon, Mexico, and Brazil. Many are mistaken for cacti by those who do not know that a plant without aereoles cannot be a cactus.

The two *Euphorbias* most commonly asked about are *Euphorbia splendens* (crown-of-thorns) and *Euphorbia lactea* (milk-striped euphorbia). The former bears gray-green heavily spined stems, oblong leaves about 1 inch long, and tiny flowers which are normally pink-red, though yellow- and salmon-flowered varieties may be found. Plants generally reach about 4 feet in height. The crown-of-thorns may drop leaves at varying times during the year, especially during winter. From late spring through summer new foliage develops to replace the foliage that was lost.

The milk-striped euphorbia, which is candelabra shaped, reaches a height of 10 feet in the wild but is usually sold in sizes under 3 feet. Its angular stems are marked with white and edged with stout spines. When cut, all *Euphorbias* exude a white milky sap from leaves and stems, which causes a poison-ivy-like reaction or eye irritation upon contact. You must take great care in pruning and propagation.

FEROCACTUS (BARREL CACTUS), CACTUS FAMILY: These natives of California, Texas, and Mexico are extremely popular with collectors. The barrel cacti are usually densely clothed in colorful spines which contrast beautifully with the large, bright-hued flowers born at the tops of the plants. Most are rounded or oval, but they may also be cylindrical. The majority of specimens sold are less than a foot in height and diameter.

KLEINIA (GOOSEBERRY KLEINIA, STRING-OF-BEADS), COMPOSITE FAMILY: *Kleinias* are a group of succulents highly diverse in habit of growth and geographic origin. They are represented in most amateur succulent collections by one of two rather novel species: *Kleinia herreianus* (gooseberry kleinia) and *Kleinia rowleyana* (string-of-beads). Both have hanging stems lined with little green "beads," about ½ inch long, which are actually leaves. These plants are ideal for hanging containers, where their stems cascade freely. The gooseberry kleinia has multiple translucent stripes on its leaves; the string-of-beads has a single translucent band.

LITHOPS (LIVING STONES), MESEMBRYANTHEMUM FAMILY: There are approximately forty species and one hundred varieties of these southern African natives, all of which closely resemble highly polished stones—

hence their common name. I just love them. *Lithops* produce two thick semi-circular leaves, flat on top, which grow to a diameter of about 3 inches. The leaves are separated by a narrow cleft from which new leaves grow, a pair at a time. The old pair of leaves withers and dies some time after the new pair is produced, and on it goes. Proportionately large white or yellow daisy-like blossoms arise from the cleft, and it is only during flowering that *Lithops* look anything like living plants. The tops of the leaves are colored and patterned in various shades of brown, gray, beige, green, and red—depending on variety.

MAMMILLARIA (PINCUSHION CACTUS), CACTUS FAMILY: There are over one hundred and fifty species of *Mammillarias* hailing from Mexico and the United States. They are among the mainstays of the cactus garden be-cause, unlike many cacti, they flower when young and are relatively easy to grow. Some produce a single, rounded stem, others cluster freely; some are covered with long white hairs, hooks, and stiff or soft spines. Plant color varies with species and variety. All *Mammillarias* have in common the absence of spined ribs and the presence of spine-tipped protuberances all over their stems, hence the nickname pincushion. During spring, *Mammillarias* produce a garland of white, yellow, pink, or magenta flowers, depending on variety, around the tops of the stems. Flowers are followed by long-lasting fleshy red fruits which some people claim are very tasty—I have never given them a try.

OPUNTIA (BUNNY EARS, PAPER SPINE), CACTUS FAMILY: Opuntias, native to arid regions of the New World, are among the most commonly grown and well-known cacti. Two species most often asked about are *Opuntia microdasys* (bunny ears) and *Opuntia glomerata* (paper spine). The former bears flattened pads, 3–6 inches high, on plants that reach a height of about 3 feet. Tufts of tiny bristles, yellow, white, or rust colored, depending on variety, are closely spaced all over the pads. These bristles are easily imbedded in the skin, causing irritation, though you may hardly feel them go in. They are not hard to remove; just scrub with soap and a soft brush. The paper spine produces rounded oblong segments, a dull green color, covered with 1–4-inch, flesh-colored papery spines plus tufts of bristles.

SANSEVIERIA (SPEAR SANSEVIERIA, HAHN'S SANSEVIERIA), LILY FAM-ILY: Few plants are as dependable, forgiving, and carefree as the sansevierias, plants that I once heard a colleague say would grow in a closet. This is a bit of an overstatement, but these plants do require less light to survive than most succulents and you do have to work rather hard to kill one. The two types most commonly found are *Sansevieria cylindrica* (spear san-sevieria) and *Sansevieria trifasciata hahnii* (Hahn's sansevieria). The former bears stiff, dark green leaves, up to 5 feet long and 1½ inches wide, which are interestingly marked. Hahn's sansevieria produces a rosette of leathery leaves, about 6 inches high, resembling the top of a pineapple. The leaves are either marked with grayish bands or have wide yellow margins, depending on variety.

Availability

With the exception of the Christmas cactus and kalanchoes, a wide variety of succulents is available throughout the year. Most sources carry the more common types including those I have described. If you want something unusual, you will probably have to shop by mail. The appendix lists several nurseries that ship plants throughout the country.

Selection

There are hundreds of succulents found in the trade, and the criteria that make each a specimen worthy of purchase are different. The best judgements are made only after examining the succulent collections in botanic gardens and nurseries and those of hobbyists who grow large groups of plants. Then you will be familiar with the qualities exhibited by well-grown specimens and will be able to spot a plant subjected to cultural malpractice from yards away. Until then, watch out for the following:

• The stems of columnar-type cacti should be approximately the same diameter from top to bottom; they should not taper off or bulge out at any point, especially towards the tip—an indication that the plant has been grown under lower than optimum light levels or higher than recommended temperatures during one or more growing season.

• Succulents should not require staking to stay upright unless they are extremely large. The need for staking may indicate that the root system is insufficient to support the plant, or that the plant has just been propagated and is not really ready for sale.

• Avoid buying succulents with soft, water-soaked, or brown areas on the stems—indications of a fungus or rot problem. Look especially closely at the point where the stem meets the soil line.

• Branched succulents like the jade plant should be stocky and compact, not sparse or thin looking—indications of poor treatment, probably too little light.

• The spines on new cactus growth are generally softer than those on older parts of the plant. Check to see if your plant has made recent growth or was neglected and did not grow at all during the last growing season.

• Species that sucker freely, like the *Aloes*, should be potted in containers large enough to accommodate the mother plant and her progeny.

Plants should not be hanging over the edge of the pot or be precariously situated in the container.

• The foliage and stems of succulents should be plump and firm, not shrivelled or puckered—indications of a moisture problem, either too much or too little.

• The spines on armored succulents should not be damaged, nor should the plant itself be seriously marred—indications of neglect or rough handling.

Cultural Requirements

Succulents need high light intensity to achieve their natural shape, form, and color. Without it they stretch, droop, and fade. With a sunny spot, you are in business. In a dark apartment or a house situated on a heavily shaded lot, your chances of success are limited, and you must supplement the natural light with artificial light. Other requirements for success are easy to meet. On balance, these plants require very little to thrive, flower, and provide you with a special display the year-round.

LIGHT: The majority of succulents require at least 4 hours of direct sunlight each day. Place plants in front of the sunniest window in your home, preferably one that faces south, southeast, or east. The window should be unobstructed. Natural light is preferred, but if there is not a sunny window in your home, the existing sunlight can be supplemented with artificial light.

The best artificial light is fluorescent. A standard 4-foot fixture equipped with two 40-watt tubes—one cool white and one warm white—is ideal. A 4-foot, four-tube fixture equipped with cool and warm tubes arranged alternately is even better. Set plants 6–12 inches from the light source if you are using only fluorescents. If the light fixture is a supplement to natural light, it can be placed higher above the plants.

You can also supplement existing natural light with incandescent lamps. They emit a more attractive light, better suited for living areas, but are not as energy efficient or beneficial to plants. Incandescent lamps can be mounted in the ceiling or wall 4–6 feet above the plant stand. They should not be too close to plants because they create excessive heat, which can cause damage. Alone, incandescent light is not suitable for plant growth.

Plants that are not getting enough light stretch out and become misshapen. This is especially true of cacti, whose stems decrease in diameter, permanently destroying the natural form. Other succulents may become so leggy that staking is required. Also, plants grown under lower than optimum light levels are unlikely to flower. Succulents should be given a quarter turn every week or so to prevent them from leaning toward the light source.

TEMPERATURE: Most succulents grow best when temperatures from spring through fall are 60–65° F. at night and 5–15 degrees higher during the day; winter temperatures should be 45–55° F. at night, with day temperatures anywhere from 60 to 80° F. Cool winter nights are essential to initiate flower formation and to assure a proper growth habit. Higher than recommended night temperatures during winter may cause plants to grow too rapidly and become leggy specimens uncharacteristic of their species.

MOISTURE: When to water is the most frequently asked question about succulents, and improper watering results in the loss of more plants than any other factor. Each grower must learn this skill from firsthand experience and a little experimenting with plants in his or her own environment. The advice provided is derived from my success with succulents grown in the natural light of a southeast-facing window.

I have always watered succulents other than cacti when the top *half* of soil in the container feels completely dry to the touch. Then, as always, I water thoroughly. During winter you may find that the soil dries at a different rate than at other times of the year.

Cacti require less water than other pot plants, to be sure, but like all living things they require moisture to survive. The key is balance. My experience is that cacti in the home are generally killed by a *lack* of moisture rather than too much. This is the result of the popular notion that cacti do not need any water or water only in infinitesimal amounts. In the wild, cacti develop long roots that can absorb water from deep within the earth. Therefore, periods of drought, even extended, find cacti thriving and flowering. In a container, the story is different—the roots have nowhere to go in search of water, and regular replenishment is necessary.

The advice that follows reflects my regimen for watering cacti, none of which are epiphytes. Epiphytic cacti should be watered as you would a Christmas cactus, described on page 92.

Summer: During the dog days, water cacti when the top layer of soil in the container feels completely dry to the touch. Then water thoroughly until water runs through the drainage holes in the bottom of the container. Wait 15 minutes and discard any excess water that has accumulated in the drip plate beneath the container. My cacti require water about every 10 days during summer.

Autumn: As day length begins to decrease and cooler days replace hot ones, the top layer of soil dries less frequently between waterings. Begin watering when the top *half* of the soil in the pot feels completely dry. With my plants this occurs about every 2½ weeks from mid to late fall unless temperatures and light intensity are unusually high.

Winter: During the short cloudy days of winter, cacti should be watered only enough to prevent them from shrivelling. Too much water at this time will cause plants to grow too quickly and stretch out of shape. It may also prevent flowering. Watering thoroughly about every 4 weeks usually works well, but you must examine your plants. Check for signs of shrivelling to be sure you have not waited too long between waterings.

Spring: New growth begins in spring, and an adequate water supply must be provided at this time. As days lengthen, temperatures rise, and light intensity increases, plants will begin growing, and you must return to watering when the top *layer* of soil feels dry—as you did in summer. New cactus growth is usually lighter in color than the last year's growth, and the newly developed spines are softer than those on older plant parts. Some growers put a tiny ink mark at the top of the plant in winter, and as soon as they see growth above the mark they know it is time to increase watering frequency. This is a great trick.

FERTILIZER: Every succulent fancier will give you different advice on when to fertilize and how much fertilizer to apply. With cacti what works well for me is the application of a high-phosphorus fertilizer, the water-soluble type, with an analysis of 15–30–15. I apply it at half strength every month from the time new growth appears in spring through mid-autumn. I withhold fertilizer for the rest of the year.

With the other succulents, like *Aloe, Agave*, or the jade plant, I fertilize once a month with the same product. I apply the fertilizer at full strength from mid-March through mid-November. Some succulent lovers may take issue with these schedules, but I have done quite well with them after much trial and error.

PLACEMENT IN THE HOME: Succulents must be given ample light throughout the year and cool growing temperatures during winter. If you provide these conditions and an appropriate water supply, your plants should reward you with some of the most beautiful and unusual flowers imaginable. When plants are in bloom, feel free to take them off the window-sill or out from under the lights and set them on a coffee table or wherever they are sure to be noticed and appreciated. Getting a succulent to bloom is the result of your dedicated efforts—you deserve all the compliments these plants are sure to receive.

POTTING AND SOIL: A soil mix that works well for most succulents contains equal parts of packaged potting soil and a coarse grade of builder's sand—the type with little pieces of gravel scattered throughout. Depending on plant size, I mix a teaspoon to a tablespoon of bone meal into the volume of mix placed in the bottom half of the pot. Bone meal is a slow-release fertilizer which supplements the water-soluble chemical product recommended above.

131

A spiny succulent is not a joy to repot, for obvious reasons, and people tend to put off this essential chore way beyond the point of necessity. Like every other plant, succulents need fresh soil and more room as they grow. Many hobbyists repot all their succulent plants each spring in containers that are ½ inch larger in diameter than the old ones, 1 inch larger for really big specimens like *Agaves* and *Euphorbias*.

I generally repot cacti every 2 years, increasing pot size by ½ inch—1 inch for big plants. My other succulents are repotted when I see roots growing through the drainage holes, when the soil dries more quickly than usual between waterings, when water runs through the soil faster than in the past, or when plants have made rapid growth since their last repotting. Select a new container ½–1 inch larger than the old one, depending on plant size. I will also repot, regardless of other factors, when the potting soil has begun to feel and look compacted or muddy, which happens as it breaks down. If your plant needs fresh soil but does not require a larger container, you can remove some of the old medium from the top of the soil mass and replace it with fresh soil.

I have seen scores of tips in books on how to repot the armored succulents without impaling yourself. None of this advice seems to work for me. If I make a paper sling and place it around the plant, I end up dropping the plant and breaking some spines. If I trick my husband into assisting me, invariably we both get stuck. Generally, I fight fire with fire. I put on a pair of heavy rubber household gloves, then a pair of heavy duty garden gloves, and work slowly and carefully. After I have finished, I always put the gloves in the washing machine because tiny cactus bristles, especially those of the *Opuntias*, become imbedded in the gloves. You really want to get them out before you redon those gloves—believe me. Other than the need to protect your hands, the principles of repotting succulents are the same as for any other plant.

PRUNING: Cacti have a natural shape, form, and habit which generally should not be tampered with by pruning. However, if a cactus becomes too tall for the available space, it may be necessary to cut the plant back.

• To prune a cactus that produces jointed pads, like the *Opuntias*, make a clean cut with a sharp knife at the joint.

• The leaves of rosette-forming succulents, like *Aloes* and *Echeverias*, occasionally yellow and die. These leaves should be cut off close to the stem of the plant with a sharp knife. I am always breaking off the leaves of my *Aloe* for use on minor cuts or burns. This does disfigure the plant, but if you use pieces of the older lower leaves, it will not look too bad.

• Shrub-like succulents, such as the jade plant, should be pruned regularly by pinching the growing tips at a node, the point where a leaf joins the stem. This will encourage and promote a fuller, more bushy habit. Jade plants are also pruned for purposes of shaping, sometimes to form a plant with a bare trunk and foliage at the top. This creates a tree-like effect that is extremely attractive. Just cut the bottom growth off as close to the trunk as possible so that stubs are not left along the bare trunk.

Propagation

Succulents can be propagated at any season in one of four ways, depending on the plant's habit of growth. You can take tip cuttings, stem cuttings, or leaf cuttings, or you can divide plants—separating offsets from the mother plant. All succulents can also be propagated from seed.

Tip cuttings are taken from multi-stemmed plants such as the jade. Simply cut off a 3–4-inch piece from the end of any healthy vigorous stem. Make the cut above a node. Allow the end of the cutting to form a callous by letting it sit out overnight on a paper towel. Then insert the cutting in moistened vermiculite, exactly as described for kalanchoes on page 87. Once rooted, pot individually in 3-inch containers or plant small groups of newly rooted cuttings in a larger pot.

Taking *stem cuttings* from leafless cacti or other succulents, like the *Cereus* cacti or *Euphorbias*, will permanently mar the plant. However, it is the only way to vegetatively (asexually) propagate them at home. New growth will not occur at the cut, though stems may branch at a point beneath where the cut was made. The best stem cuttings are taken from the tips of vigorous plants that are not in bloom. Cut a 4–6-inch piece of the stem. Then allow it to callous by leaving it out on a paper towel for 24 to 48 hours. Plant the cutting in its permanent pot, which you have filled with the mix recommended on page 131. It may require staking to stay upright. You can use small bamboo stakes or popsicle sticks for this purpose. Keep the medium evenly moist but never soggy. Allow the top layer to dry thoroughly between waterings. Once the cutting is established in its container, begin watering as described on page 130. Choose a pot that leaves ½ inch on all sides between the newly cut stem and the inner walls of the pot. Leave the mother plant in its container to continue growing.

Leaf cuttings are taken from certain succulents which, unlike most plants, can be grown from a single leaf. *Crassulas* and *Echeverias* are easily propagated in this manner. Literally thousands of new plants can be generated from a single specimen. Take an entire leaf and insert the bottom half in a clear plastic box filled halfway to the top with moistened vermiculite. Place a lid on the box. Tiny plants will appear at the base of the mother leaf. Once they are a manageable size, pot each one separately in 2–3-inch pots.

Succulents that produce offsets, tiny plants around the base of the mother plant, can be *divided. Echeverias, Aloes,* and *Agaves* are easily

133

propagated by offsets. The easiest way to divide succulents is to unpot the mother plant along with her progeny, which are attached to her by some type of underground stem. Snip off the suckers you wish to grow separately. Pot the young offsets in suitably sized containers filled with the recommended mix. Baby them along for several weeks after potting by setting them on a pebble tray or placing them under a plastic tent, as described on page 147. In the meantime, repot the mother plant—she is sure to reproduce again.

Seeds can be rooted as described for kalanchoes on page 87. There are sources of a wide variety of seeds listed in the appendix.

FOLIAGE PLANTS

Backbone of the Indoor Garden

Scientific Name: Various
Origin: Widespread, mostly tropical

With the exception of ferns, mosses, lichens, and other lower plants, all plants flower. It is the flowers that host a plant's reproductive system, affording each species the opportunity to continue in its natural form for eternity. Without the flower (and discounting human intervention), plants would be a one-shot deal. For this reason, the term "foliage plant" is actually a misnomer, and the common belief that foliage plants do not flower, erroneous. In their native habitats, the lovely philodendrons and ever popular kentia palm bloom as regularly as the most glamorous "flowering plants."

The aesthetic value of foliage plants stems from ornamental leaves rather than dramatic or colorful flowers. The blossoms are often quite insignificant in appearance, particularly in contrast to the foliage. At the same time, foliage plants are the backbone of the vast majority of indoor gardens. They provide substance and depth to any collection, no matter how spectacular the flowering varieties displayed nearby. In addition, foliage plants are a mainstay of the ornamental-plant industry, and little wonder — they are beautiful the year-round, and there is no fear of flower failure.

There are foliage plants to suit every taste and each person you know. There are plants for the novice as well as the sophisticated collector of exotic tropicals — even for the friend who kills plants with alarming regularity. The challenge is to select the right plant for the right person.

Descriptions

Of the hundreds of different foliage plants that make their way into American homes, most can be divided into three categories: vines, upright pot plants, and large specimens or accent plants. All serve the owner in a special way and with less bother than most flowering species.

VINES: Vining plants are those that produce long, pendant stems. They generally grow very quickly and are suitable for indoor gardeners who want the gratification of a full plant as soon as possible. Vines are ideally suited to hanging containers, where their stems can cascade gracefully over the wall of the pot. None are particularly difficult to grow, all tolerate some adversity, and in general they are wise choices for the casual gardener on your shopping list. Listed here are the most popular and frequently asked about vines.

Cissus rhombifolia (**grape ivy**): Shiny three-lobed leaves, 4 inches long and 3–4 inches wide, start out a bronze color, then turn deep green. They are carefree and cooperative to train.

Gynura sarmentosa (**purple passion vine**): Exotic 3–4-inch leaves are purple underneath and thickly covered with purple fuzz. For all this uniqueness, purple passion vines are no more demanding than the more ordinary fare.

Hedera helix (**English ivy**): English ivy is a handsome hanging plant, especially the small-leaved varieties, which may have bird's-foot- or heart-shaped foliage, and the variegated forms, which have white or cream-colored markings. Watch out for spider mites, a pest with a real affinity for *Hedera*.

Philodendron cordatum (**heart-leaved philodendron**): The heart-leaved philodendron your grandmother grew on her kitchen window-sill is still an all-time favorite. Few other plants have more rich satiny green leaves or are more reliable.

Plectranthus australis (**Swedish ivy**): Swedish ivy leaves, about 1 inch across, display the freshest green color available. Under proper conditions they are produced extremely rapidly. The variegated form, green leaves marked white, though slightly slower growing, are even prettier.

Scindapsus aureus (**pothos**): Gorgeous specimens of pothos, a plant closely resembling and related to the heart-leaved philodendron, are found thriving in the collections of the most inept gardeners. The most commonly grown forms have leaves marbled white or yellow.

Zebrina species (**wandering Jew**): The wandering Jew is a beautiful genus of plants, which includes some spectacularly colored forms, most bearing leaves 3 inches long and about 1½ inches wide. Foliage is striped red, white, silvery green, and/or purple depending on variety. They are easy to care for and grow quickly.

UPRIGHT POT PLANTS: The term "upright pot plants" is a makeshift description of species generally grown or sold in 3–6-inch pots. They are not all upright; many of these plants produce arching leaves or stems. Though the ultimate size of many upright pot plants is quite large, and mature specimens could easily be used as accent plants, most found in cultivation are windowsill or coffee table size. The following plants were the twelve most asked about during my years at the U.S. Botanic Garden. These plants tolerate average indoor conditions beautifully.

Aglaonema species (**Chinese evergreen**): The lance-shaped leaves of the most commonly grown Chinese evergreens are 6–12 inches long and 2–3 inches wide. They are born around a stem 2–3 feet high. The foliage may be plain green or beautifully marked with cream, light green, or silvery designs. Chinese evergreens retain their rich markings in relatively low light levels.

Asparagus species **(asparagus fern):** The big surprise is that the well-known asparagus ferns are really members of the lily family. The species offered in the trade are covered with delicate needle-like structures called phylloclades, which perform the same botanical function as leaves. Asparagus ferns thrive in higher light intensities than most people provide.

Begonia species **(rex begonia, angel wing or cane-stemmed begonia):** You are sure to find a begonia to suit any taste, since these plants are remarkably diverse in size, habit, and color. Most require high humidity and tender loving care. The rex begonias are valued for their highly colored, intricately detailed leaf patterns. The angel wings are noted for striking foliage, a handsome habit, and the extra bonus of delicate flowers, which are produced in abundance on many varieties.

Chamadorea elegans **(parlor palm):** Parlor palms stay under 2 feet in height with fronds up to 1 foot long. I think they look best when potted in decorative ceramic containers. They are prone to spider mite infestation and must be sprayed forcefully with tap water every few weeks to discourage these nuisances.

Chlorophytum comosum **(spider plant, airplane plant):** The gracefully arching leaves of the familiar spider plant are up to 16 inches long and 1 inch wide. The most commonly grown form has a prominent white stripe down the center of the leaves. Novice gardeners often allow the soil to become bone dry between waterings, a practice that contributes to browning of the leaf tips and produces cracks in the center of the leaves.

Coleus blumei **(coleus):** Choose coleus if you are looking for spectacular color from a foliage plant. The range of combinations seems endless and includes multiple shades of purple, pink, and green, or bright green and maroon. This member of the mint family bears pointed leaves up to 4 inches long on plants up to 4 feet high, though specimens under 18 inches are far more common. Frequent pruning is a must for well-branched, bushy specimens.

Maranta species **(prayer plants):** Leaves of the prayer plant become erect at night, reminiscent of praying hands, and resume a horizontal position during the day. There are different species, most of which grow about 8 inches high and twice that wide, bearing oval leaves about 4 inches long. The foliage is gorgeously marked with linear patterns or is colorfully spotted. Leaf edges may turn crisp if humidity is too low.

Nephrolepis exaltata bostoniensis **(Boston fern):** The Boston fern has graceful stems, up to 5 feet long, which are densely clothed in delicate leaflets. The best specimens are grown in cool rooms and are provided with bright indirect light. There is a wide range of cultivated varieties that produce frilly leaflets, leaflets of varying size, and shorter stems.

Peperomia species **(peperomia):** The leaves of the most popular peperomias are fascinatingly corrugated, handsomely marked (in one species like a watermelon rind), or marbled cream and yellow. They require brighter light and slightly drier soil than most people provide.

Philodendron species **(philodendron):** There are about two hundred philodendrons and countless varieties, including types with leaves that are red underneath, variegated white, lobed, or oddly shaped. Some are climbers, others are upright. Generally, the less well-known types are as easy to grow as the common heart-leaved philodendron. Keep an eye out for the novelty philodendrons—they make great choices for the serious collector of tropicals.

Spathiphyllum clevelandii **(spathiphyllum):** The spathiphyllum is one of my favorites. It has long-stalked leaves up to 18 inches long and 4 inches wide and is handsome as well as fast growing. In relatively low light it produces an exotic-looking, white, petal-like spathe behind an odd-looking tubular spadix, characteristics of the aroid family to which this plant belongs. What a deal!

Tolmiea menziesii **(piggyback plant):** The fuzzy-leaved piggyback plant, about 8 inches high and twice that wide, carries its progeny perched oddly at the leaf bases. The leaf edges may turn crisp from insufficient humidity and lack of light. To maintain the piggyback a pebble tray is a must, as is a position by a sunny window.

ACCENT PLANTS: Accent plants are those large plants frequently used alone as accents to interior decor. In the wild, these plants grow too big for the average home; however, in cultivation, they generally retain manageable sizes for quite some time. Though it is common to find windowsill-sized subjects of the plants described, you are just as likely to see far larger varieties offered for sale. If you are looking for a big plant, one of the ten choices listed here is sure to suit your fancy. You generally pay dearly for a large foliage house plant—choose wisely.

Araucaria heterophylla **(Norfolk Island pine):** The Norfolk Island pine, a beautiful, graceful, and much admired accent plant, is described in detail on pages 82–83.

Brassaia actinophylla **(schefflera, umbrella tree):** The ever popular schefflera, generally 3–6 feet high, is among nature's most gracefully shaped subjects. Its leaflets, each up to 12 inches long and 3 inches wide, are arranged in an umbrella-like whorl, hence one of its nicknames. The schefflera is so prone to spider mites that I sometimes wonder if it is worth the effort required to keep these pests at bay. Spray your plant forcefully with tap water every few weeks to reduce dryness and help prevent infestation.

Codiaeum variegatum pictum **(croton):** There are dozens of croton varieties found in the trade, with an almost infinite number of exotic color combinations and foliage patterns. Foliage shapes vary from flat, lance-shaped blades to twisted leaves resembling corkscrews. Plants are generally in the 3–5-foot range. To retain their rich hues crotons must be given adequate light. You can prevent lower leaf drop, a common complaint, by the use of a pebble tray.

Cycas species **(cycads):** Cycads are ancient cone-bearing plants that resemble palms but are actually related to pines, firs, and spruces. Cycads similar to those available today existed before dinosaurs roamed the earth. In the wild, plants grow as large as palms, but most pot-grown specimens are under 5 feet high and bear leathery fronds 2–3 feet long. Cycads may cost more than most specimens, but they are well worth it.

Dieffenbachia species **(dieffenbachia, dumb cane):** Dieffenbachias have beautifully marked foliage; patterns and colors vary with species. Pot-grown plants are usually under 5 feet high, with leaves up to 24 inches long and 8 inches wide. People complain about lower leaf drop, an unavoidable phenomenon as plants grow taller. Bright indirect light is essential to keep the markings clear and to prevent the need for staking. The nickname dumb cane derives from the fact that the sap found in this plant's leaves and stems contains an irritant known as calcium oxylate, which, if swallowed, affects the larynx, causing temporary speechlessness. It's true—don't try it.

Dizygotheca elegantisima **(false aralia):** This graceful and fragile-looking plant, about 6 feet high, bears leaves composed of about ten thin, jagged leaflets, each approximately 5 inches long. The leaves start out bronze but turn a rich dark green. This plant tends to drop leaves unexpectedly. Increasing humidity by the use of a pebble tray may help prevent this problem.

Dracaena species **(dracaena, corn plant):** The two dracaenas most frequently asked about are *Dracaena marginata*, which produces a cluster of red-margined leaves up to 15 inches long and ½ inch wide atop a thin, notched stem about 6 feet tall; and *Dracaena fragrans massangeana,* the corn plant, which reaches about the same height and bears leaves ultimately 30 inches long and 3 inches wide, with a wide, yellow center stripe. Try increasing humidity if the leaves of either species turn crisp at the tips or along the edges.

Ficus species **(ficus, fig tree, rubber tree plant, weeping fig):** Ficus species are the most asked about foliage house plants, especially *Ficus benjamina* (weeping fig) and *Ficus elastica* (rubber tree plant). The former, usually 4–6 feet in height, bears shiny leaves up to 4 inches long on gracefully arching branches. It may drop leaves at various times during the year, but if you prune in spring, new foliage will develop to replace lost leaves. The rubber tree plant bears leathery leaves, up to 1 foot long and 6 inches wide, which may be variegated or may start out bronze and then turn green, depending on variety. This plant drops lower leaves as it matures, a phenomenon that cannot be prevented but may be slowed by increasing humidity with the use of a pebble tray.

Howeia fosteriana (**kentia palm**): If you want to buy a little bit of paradise for someone living in a colder clime, the kentia is perfect. It is tolerant of low light for long periods but thrives and grows more rapidly in sunnier spots. Kentias produce a single trunk, which in cultivation usually stays 6–8 feet tall. Many growers plant several specimens in one container, giving people the mistaken impression that it is a multi-trunked species. Watch out for spider mites, which love all the palms.

Monstera deliciosa (**monstera, cut-leaved philodendron**): A monstera growing up a bark slab is one of the indoor garden's most common sights. Check your doctor's waiting room. Its rounded, lobed, and often perforated leaves, up to 18 inches long, look like they have been given a high gloss shine. It may not be the most imaginative gift, but it is likely to perform beautifully for the less talented gardener. In fact, it may soon outgrow the space for which it was intended and have to be pruned severely or used for propagation.

Availability and Selection

With foliage plants, never settle for second choice or a weak specimen. Most plants are available year-round from a variety of stores, including supermarkets, garden centers, plant shops, and other businesses dealing in plants. You can often buy perfectly lovely foliage plants on urban street corners. The selection is as broad as your flexibility in searching for the perfect choice. Selecting a worthy specimen is not more difficult than finding one. Just keep a few points in mind.

- Foliage plants are troubled by a number of pests, notably mealybugs, spider mites, and scale insects; each is described in Part 5. Avoid presenting someone with an infested plant. Pests spread like lightning from one plant to another, and in no time at all an entire collection can be severely damaged.
- Purchase robust-looking plants. The leaves of green plants should be rich in color, not mottled or lackluster. Plants with patterned foliage should have clear markings and bright colors. The tips and edges of the leaves should not be brown—an indication of improper care.
- Plants should be potted in adequately sized containers. The pot should not be out of proportion to the plant. Roots should not be growing out of the drainage holes in the bottom of the pot, and the specimen should be centered in its container. A well-potted plant is usually one that has been properly tended.

Cultural Requirements

Most horticulturists believe that the most common mistake in foliage plant care is too much water. This error is frequently made, but my experience indicates that most plants suffer from a lack of light. While foliage plants generally require less light than plants grown for their flowers, most will not thrive, indeed survive, in a dark corner several feet from the window, on a coffee table in the center of a room, or in front of a heavily shaded window.

Another common cause of failure with foliage plants is low humidity. Most foliage plants are indigenous to moist tropical environments. The atmospheres in our homes tend to be very dry, especially during winter when the heat is on. Though a lack of humidity may not kill your plants, it will surely contribute to a lack of general vigor and result in specimens you will soon lose interest in. With a minimum of effort you can grow sensational foliage house plants, many of which can be easily propagated or given as gifts appropriate for all occasions.

LIGHT AND MOISTURE: The vast and varied selection of available foliage plants would not be served well by sweeping generalizations as to light and moisture requirements. Even specific and detailed plant-by-plant recommendations leave out the elements of judgement and horticultural horse sense crucial to maintaining a thriving foliage plant. Conditions vary from one locale to the next. The amount of light coming through an east-facing window depends not only on geography but also on how much of the light is obstructed by trees, nearby buildings, or an awning hung over the window. You must always be on the lookout for signs of too much or too little light and adjust the position of your plant accordingly.

Similarly, the frequency with which a plant requires water depends on several factors, including temperature, humidity, light intensity, container size, the type of growing medium used, and the plant's stage of growth. Watering every Tuesday or every payday can be a fatal error. You must feel the soil. Only your sense of touch can guide you correctly. Whenever plants are watered, they should be thoroughly soaked. Water should run through the drainage holes in the bottom of the pot. After 15 minutes you should discard any excess water that has accumulated in the drip plate beneath the container. Many plants grow best when humidity is high. For these species you must provide a pebble tray.

The chart on page 142 is a guide to the requirements of light and moisture for the plants I have just described. With a little common sense and the use of this chart, the odds are all in your favor.

TEMPERATURE: Most foliage plants do very well when night temperatures are 55–70° F. and day temperatures are 60–80° F. Most homes fall within these ranges, except during the hottest days of summer. Even so,

LIGHT & MOISTURE REQUIREMENTS

Scientific Name	Common Name	Light	Moisture
Aglaonema species	Chinese evergreen	Low	Moist
Araucaria heterophylla	Norfolk Island pine	High	Moist
Asparagus species	Asparagus fern	Medium	Moist
Begonia species	Begonias	Medium	Moist
Brassaia actinophylla	Schefflera, umbrella tree	Medium	Moist
Chamadorea elegans	Parlor palm	Medium	Moist
Chlorophytum comosum	Spider plant, airplane plant	Medium	Moist
Cissus rhombifolia	Grape ivy	Medium	Moist
Codiaeum variegatum pictum	Croton	High	Moist
Coleus blumei	Coleus	Medium	Wet
Cycas species	Cycads	Medium	Moist
Dieffenbachia species	Dieffenbachia, dumb cane	Medium	Moist
Dizygotheca elegantisima	False aralia	Medium	Moist
Dracaena species	Dracaena, corn plant	Medium	Moist
Ficus species	Ficus, fig tree, rubber tree plant, weeping fig	High	Dry
Gynura sarmentosa	Purple passion vine	Medium	Moist
Hedera helix	English ivy	Low	Moist
Howeia fosteriana	Kentia palm	Low	Moist
Maranta species	Prayer plant	Medium	Moist
Monstera deliciosa	Monstera, cut-leaved philodendron	Low	Moist
Nephrolepis exaltata bostoniensis	Boston fern	Medium	Wet
Peperomia species	Peperomia	High	Dry
Philodendron species	Philodendron	Low	Moist
Plectranthus australis	Swedish ivy	Medium	Moist
Scindapsus aureus	Pothos	Low	Moist
Spathiphyllum clevelandii	Spathiphyllum	Low	Moist
Tolmiea menziesii	Piggyback plant	Medium	Moist
Zebrina species	Wandering Jew	Low	Moist

High Light: Place plants within a few feet of a window that faces south or east. During summer you may have to move plants back a few feet, partially close Venetian blinds, or close sheer curtains during the sunniest part of the day to prevent foliage burn. If plants are getting too much sun, the leaves closest to the window will fade, become flaccid, and may be scorched.

Medium Light: Plants will grow well in a window that faces west or north. A southern or eastern exposure where light intensity is reduced by buildings, curtains, or trees is also good for plants in this category.

Low Light: Plants may be placed several feet from the window for long periods of time. However, if they show light deficiency symptoms, such as stretching toward the light source, faded leaf markings, or smaller than normal leaves, move them closer to a window.

Dry: Water thoroughly when the top *half* of the soil in the container feels totally dry to the touch.

Moist: Water thoroughly when the top *inch* of soil in the container feels totally dry to the touch.

Wet: Keep the soil evenly and constantly moist, but never soggy.

most foliage plants have the marvelous ability to adapt to a wide temperature range.

FERTILIZER: Foliage plants benefit greatly from the monthly application of any water-soluble chemical fertilizer recommended for use on house plants. There are scores of products available, and each is perfectly suitable as long as the directions are carefully followed. More is *not* better. Omit fertilizer during the shortest days of winter, from around Christmas through mid-March, when plants are not actively growing.

I sometimes spread a little slow-release fertilizer on top of the soil after potting, according to package directions. These slow-release products, also easily obtainable, look like tiny round beads. Every time you water, some of the coating on the beads breaks down, releasing a little bit of fertilizer into the soil. I do not use the slow-release product as a substitute for the water-soluble chemical fertilizer, but as a supplement—and with good results.

PLACEMENT IN THE HOME: Naturally, you should keep your foliage plants in areas that meet their light requirements. Also, avoid drafts from heating or cooling ducts or a door that is frequently opened.

POTTING AND SOIL: Plants need repotting when roots start growing through the drainage holes in the bottom of the pot, when the water runs through the soil faster than usual, or when the soil dries more rapidly between waterings than it has in the past. As with many flowering plants and succulents, repot foliage plants into containers that are ½ to 1 inch larger in diameter than the old pots. It really does not make much difference whether you change from clay to plastic or vice versa. A preference for one or the other is strictly personal. However, you should remember that soil in clay pots dries faster than soil in plastic or ceramic containers. I use the same simple mix for all of my foliage plants with great success. It contains 2 parts packaged potting soil and 1 part perlite.

I have received many calls from cat owners who claim that their pet uses the large containers in which accent plants are potted as a litter box. If this occurs in your home, spread a layer of pea gravel, available at most hardware stores and garden centers, over the soil surface. Cats are usually deterred by this simple measure.

PRUNING: I love to prune. Foliage plants become bushier, healthier specimens and make me feel that they love me as much as I love them. Pruning is not cruel and does not hurt the plant. It may look depressing at first, but, believe me, plants grow and renew themselves in a form that is bigger and better than before. The foliage plants I have described are pruned differently and for varying purposes. The most common pruning practices for each are described in the following paragraphs. All of these plants can be pruned at any season, except where noted.

Aralias and crotons: Both aralias and crotons benefit from regular pinching back of the growing tips, which forces branching and encourages a full, compact habit. Make all cuts just above the point where a leaf joins the stem, to avoid leaving stubs.

Begonias: The rex begonias generally grow from a rhizome which creeps along the soil surface. The tip portion of the rhizome can be separated from the back half with a sharp knife and potted separately. This will decrease plant size, improve vigor, and generate two plants from one. Cane-stemmed, or angel wing, begonias can be cut back anywhere along the main stem, as long as cuts are made at a node. Pruning will reduce size and promote branching.

Chinese evergreens: Regular grooming will keep this plant in top form. The shape of the growth can be left undisturbed.

Coleus: Coleus benefit dramatically from regularly pinching back the growing tips and removing the flower spikes. Some gardeners leave the flower spikes in place. I find them to be rather unattractive and recommend pinching them off as soon as they appear. This will enable the plant to devote all its strength to production of the colorfully marked foliage for which they are valued.

Cycads: Cycads are generally not pruned, though yellow fronds are removed as close to the main stem as possible. Even if all the leaves were removed, new ones would eventually be produced.

Dieffenbachia: The dieffenbachia can be grown as a single-stemmed specimen, or the tip can be pinched off, forcing the plant to branch. I think this decision should be made early so the plant can be pruned while it is still small. That way, branches are produced closer to the base of the plant, not at the top.

Dracaenas: These plants generally are not pruned except for grooming. They have a natural shape and habit, which is best left undisturbed. This is not to suggest that pruning will harm them. In fact, it will probably force branching below where the cut was made. But the natural shape of dracaenas is difficult to improve upon—why try?

Ferns: Asparagus ferns and Boston ferns that are in need of a total overhaul can be sheared off at the soil line. This may seem a bit drastic, but it is the only way to produce an attractive specimen from a miserable-looking one. After shearing, return the plant to its growing area and water when the top layer of soil feels dry. If your ferns are not in need of *total* rejuvenation, simply cut off any yellow or brown growth as it appears. Many people cut off the aerial roots of the Boston fern; these are the structures that hang from the bottom of the plant and look like leafless stems. I think this is a mistake. The aerial roots absorb moisture from the air. They are a natural part of the plant, helping it to function normally, and they should be left alone.

Ficus: The most spectacular ficus plants are those that are pruned regularly to promote branching. When cut, the stems exude a white, milky sap which is harmless though messy. The stems may ooze the sap for several hours, but it can be cleaned off the plant with a damp cloth. The weeping fig particularly benefits from pruning, which forces new growth to replace the leaves shed at other times during the year. The rubber tree plant also looks best when pruned. Pruning results in branched specimens, which I think are far more attractive than single-stemmed plants.

Monsteras: Monsteras, like philodendrons, are cut back to keep plants within bounds and to encourage fullness. To keep plants tidy, yellow or brown leaves should be removed as soon as they appear.

Palms: Palms must never be cut back. They grow from a single point known as the terminal bud, which if cut or destroyed will result in the death of the plant. Yellow or brown fronds should be removed as they appear by cutting them off as close to the main stem as possible.

Peperomias: Peperomias produce a cluster of long-stalked leaves. Generally, the only cutting done is to remove a yellow or brown leaf, which can be cut off as close to the soil line or main stem as possible.

Philodendrons: Philodendrons can be cut back to keep plants within bounds and to encourage fullness.

Piggyback plants: The most interesting aspect of this plant is the piggybacked perching of the babies. Groom as needed but leave the natural form undisturbed.

Prayer plants: You can shorten the stems of prayer plants to keep them within bounds and to promote a fuller habit. If an overhaul is needed, prayer plants can be sheared off at the soil line like asparagus and Boston ferns. After shearing, water when the top soil layer feels very dry to the touch. Soon these plants will produce new leaves which emerge from the soil in tight rolls and slowly unfurl. Even well-cared-for prayer plants eventually begin to look shaggy and will be rejuvenated by this treatment. Late autumn is the best time to shear; new growth should appear by early spring.

Schefflera: These plants are not generally pruned. They have a natural shape and habit which should be left undisturbed. As always, yellow or brown leaves should be promptly removed as close to the main stem as possible.

Spathiphyllum: These plants are not generally pruned. However, yellow or brown leaves should be cut off as soon as they appear.

Spider plants: Spider plants are not usually pruned, though some growers cut off the baby spiders which are produced on runners from the mother plant. They claim the runners sap the mother's energy and that she will grow faster without them. This may be true, but I grow beautiful spider plants with all the babies left in place. I think they are the nicest thing about these plants. Brown leaf tips occur on even the healthiest spiders; these can simply be cut off with a pair of scissors. Likewise, cracked leaves can be cut off behind where they have broken. Proper watering practices should help prevent both of these problems.

Vining plants: The vining plants should be pinched back several times each year to promote a bushy habit—do not be satisfied with long, scraggly vines. Simply cut off each stem tip just above the point where a leaf joins the stem. The farther back on the stem you cut, the farther back the stem will branch. Specimens in need of serious rejuvenation should be cut back to within a few inches of the soil line. You will be amazed at the results. There is no plant less impressive than a long, skinny vine— and nothing lovelier than a full, lush, trailing plant.

Propagation

Foliage plants are among the easiest to propagate, and some of the species I have described reproduce quickly. In fact, with spider plants and the vining species, you can have a newly propagated gift ready for delivery in 4 to 6 weeks. You can't beat that. Foliage plants are vegetatively (asexually) propagated in one of four ways: tip cuttings, leaf cuttings, division, and air layering. None of these methods is difficult to master, and most people, myself included, get a big kick out of producing a dozen plants where there was only one before. If you have never propagated anything, start with tip cuttings. They are the most foolproof way to multiply foliage house plants.

All of the plants I have described can also be propagated by seed, though seeds of certain species may be hard to find. For seed sources, see the appendix.

TIP CUTTINGS: Of the foliage plants I have described, those commonly propagated by tip cuttings are: angel wing begonia, prayer plant, coleus, croton, dieffenbachia, ficus, monstera, philodendron, aralia, and all of the vines. Take 3–6-inch cuttings from the tips of healthy, non-flowering branches that have recently produced new leaves. Then follow the directions for propagating kalanchoes, page 87, using a clear plastic box filled halfway to the top with moistened vermiculite. Cuttings root in 2 to 12 weeks, depending on species, season, and conditions inside your home. Cuttings can be taken at any season, but those cut in the spring often root a bit faster than those taken at other times of the year.

LEAF CUTTINGS: Leaf cuttings are the most common way to propagate the rex begonias. A healthy leaf is removed from the plant, and the veins on the underside of the leaf are slit lengthwise. The leaf is then placed, cutside down, on moist vermiculite and can be anchored at the stem with old-fashioned, open hair pins. A clear plastic box with a clear lid works beautifully for leaf cuttings. Soon, tiny plantlets will develop around the leaf margins, and these can be cut off the mother leaf once they are a manageable size. Pot newly developed plantlets separately in 3-inch containers using the soil mix recommended on page 143, and provide extra care by setting pots on a pebble tray out of direct sunlight for a few weeks.

The piggyback plant is also propagated by leaf cuttings. Simply remove a mother leaf that has produced a tiny plantlet at its base. Lay the mother leaf on moistened vermiculite, making sure it is anchored to the medium. Soon the plantlet will take root, the mother leaf will decompose, and the young, newly rooted plant can be potted separately in a 3-inch container— or groups can be planted together in a larger pot.

DIVISION: Plants commonly propagated by division are the asparagus and Boston ferns, spider plant, all the vines, peperomia, piggyback plant, spathiphyllum, aglaonemas that have produced suckers at the base of the mother plant, single-trunked palms that have been potted two or more per pot, and multi-stemmed palms. You will get a larger plant faster by division than from any other method of propagation, but the size of the parent plant is reduced severely, and it may be quite some time before it grows as large as before.

To divide, unpot the plant and cut it in half, thirds, or quarters with a sharp knife. Cut right through the plant and the root ball. Then pot each section separately in a smaller container, leaving ½–1 inch between the newly cut root ball and the inside walls of the pot. You must baby the newly divided plants for a few weeks by keeping them out of direct sunlight, placing them on a pebble tray to increase humidity, and misting with an atomizer. If plants begin wilting, enclose them in a tent made out of plastic wrap. First, place three bamboo stakes in the pot at regular intervals, being careful not to disturb the plant. Cover the stakes and the plant with plastic wrap; the stakes should keep the plastic from touching the foliage. Then tape the bottom of the plastic to the sides of the pot, so that the plant is completely enclosed.

The easiest and fastest plant to propagate is the spider plant. There is some question whether this is propagation by tip cutting or division. Whatever you call it, it is a snap. Cut off a baby spider which has been produced on the end of a runner, but leave the runner in place—it may produce another plantlet. Root the baby spider plant in a clear plastic box exactly as described on page 87. Then pot it in a 3-inch pot—or plant groups of babies in a larger container for a flashier specimen in a hurry.

AIR LAYERING: Ficus species, dieffenbachia, and dracaenas are frequently propagated by air layering, the safest way to root a large cutting. During this process, roots are forced to develop on a branch while it is still attached to the parent plant. The "cutting" is supplied with water and nutrients from the parent during the rooting process. Air layering protects against the danger that the cutting will die before roots are formed, a real problem when rooting large cuttings any other way. Plants should be air layered just after they have produced a flush of growth and three or four new leaves have formed. Leaves will continue to grow during the air layering process, and the cutting will become longer than when you started.

• Make a vertical cut about three-quarters of the way through the branch to be propagated, 6–12 inches below the growing tip. Prop the cut open with a toothpick so it will not grow back together.

• Soak a large handful of unmilled sphagnum moss in water; then squeeze out the excess moisture.

• Place the damp moss around the branch to enclose the cut. Immediately wrap the moss with clear plastic wrap and tie both ends securely with string or yarn. Make sure the seal is tight.

• Keep the plastic wrap out of direct sunlight. A sufficient root system should form in about 3 months, though time varies with species, environmental conditions, and season. You will not have to remove the plastic to check on root growth since you will be able to see roots growing though the plastic.

• When the plastic is completely filled with roots, remove it carefully, leaving the sphagnum moss in place.

• Cut the branch just below the new root ball and pot it in an adequately sized container in a mixture of 2 parts packaged potting soil and 1 part perlite.

• Place the new plant on a pebble tray out of direct light for a few weeks.

PART 5

Pests and Diseases

Bad News for Plant Gifts

Sometimes you just can't get a break. As soon as you've got your plants growing beautifully and flowering regularly, when you've got their water and fertilizer schedules down pat, a cloud of flying white insects mysteriously appears on your fragrant gardenia, strange leaf spots begin to expand on your prize-winning begonia, or a treasured ivy begins to decline miserably for no apparent reason. To your horror you realize that a gift plant, or worse, a source of plants for future giving, is in jeopardy. Pests and diseases are bad news. I regret to say I have received this news myself.

For whatever it is worth, you can take some comfort in knowing that no garden on earth, indoors or out, is forever problem-free. Pests and diseases attack the finest and most esoteric collections in supremely stylish neighborhoods, as well as the simplest specimen seemingly isolated from the world under the fluorescent light of an office worker's desk. These problems also occur in the most carefully tended public gardens and conservatories, despite the watchful presence of professionals who examine the plants continually.

People seem to be more familiar with the insects than with plant diseases and often mistake the symptoms of one for the other. Worse, they mistake a disease-related problem for one resulting from improper care. Inaccurate diagnoses frequently result in improper and ineffective treatment. It is important to realize that pest infestation is entirely different from plant infection, and the symptoms of either may mimic what is actually the result of an error in care. *Infested* plants are host to insects or mites; *infected* plants are plagued by a fungus, virus, or bacterial disease; problems resulting from *cultural* errors are caused by improper combinations of light, water, and temperature.

149

Infested plants can be successfully treated with products and tools commonly found at home—if the problem is caught early. Infected plants are usually more difficult to "cure" and sometimes call for the use of chemicals, but success is a distinct possibility with early detection. Improper care, the cause of most plant mortalities, simply calls for getting the plant on the right cultural track. The trick is distinguishing among problems and identifying the specific malady.

While at the Botanic Garden, I was telephoned daily by plant owners sincerely upset over a declining specimen, certain the cause was an insect or disease. Frequently, callers could not wait to ask, "What can I spray?" I wince at the quantity of hazardous chemicals released into the environment because of a problem that is the result of improper watering or a lack of adequate light. It is equally pointless to spray an insecticide on a fungus-infected plant. Insecticides do not control plant diseases, and chemicals used to control diseases do not help pest-infested plants.

There are two keys to a healthy indoor garden. One is employing a few preventive techniques which can help avoid problems altogether. The other is the ability to accurately identify pests and diseases as soon as they occur. Small insect populations and minor infections are far more likely to be eradicated than more serious maladies.

Protecting Plant Gifts

While plant disorders resulting from pests and diseases cannot be entirely prevented, the frequency and severity of these problems can be reduced. Preventive actions and a watchful eye constitute the best defense against the loss of your plants. I adhere to the following regimen for all my plants, and I highly recommend it to you.

• Carefully examine new additions to your collection. The introduction of one sick plant to a perfectly healthy group can spell doom in short order. Make sure your new arrival is vigorous and healthy. Carefully examine leaves and stems for anything out of the ordinary.

• Isolate your gift for a while. I realize this is a lot to ask of someone who has just received a spectacular blooming plant. But it is a wise idea. Newly acquired specimens may harbor pests or have a problem that is not apparent at first, even upon careful scrutiny, but can appear within a week or two.

• Regularly examine all your specimens. For all your tender loving care and protectiveness, problems will still arise. It is nice to know that early detection as the result of close and careful examinations usually ends in a successful cure. Problems that have progressed to the point where they can be detected from across the room are likely to be beyond effective control measures. Look for the presence of insects or mites with a magnifying glass. Take a close look at leaf undersides where most pests feed. Anything moving does not belong. Check for disease by looking for any discolored blotches or spots on foliage, a powdery mold on any plant part, rotten or soft spots at the base of plant stems, and discolorations or a yellow and green mosaic pattern on the leaves.

• Keep plants and their environment clean. Assuming cultural requirements are met, this is the simplest and best advice for maintaining healthy plants. Regularly wash the surfaces on which plants are displayed; remove fallen plant debris to eliminate potential feeding stations for insects and disease-causing organisms. Give your plants a shower every month or so with plain tap water—do not forget the undersides of leaves where most pests feed. Give newly washed plants plenty of room in a well-ventilated place so they will dry quickly; then return them to the growing area. Use clean containers for potting; dirty clay pots can harbor all kinds of problems. Keep your tools clean; they touch all of your plants at one time or another. Wash your hands before handling plants; viruses are easily spread from one specimen to another by human hands.

• Use a sterilized growing medium. Soil taken from the garden and used for potting without prior sterilization may harbor insects, disease pathogens, and weed seeds. What could be more insulting than weeds sprouting around a newly repotted gift? (Also, garden soil is often high in clay content, which impedes drainage. Excessive moisture leads to root disorders, which can severely weaken a plant, leaving it vulnerable to attack.) I make regular purchases of pre-sterilized packaged potting soil and rarely use garden soil. Though this is more expensive, it saves an awful lot of trouble in the long run.

• Give your plants room. Adequate spacing improves ventilation, reducing the chances of infestation or infection. It also protects against inadvertently splashing water on the leaves, which encourages the spread of fungus diseases and may cause spotting and discoloration on fuzzy-leaved species such as African violets.

• Toss out plants with serious problems. Why risk an entire collection by exposing it to one ailing plant? If discarding a once-glorious specimen is too painful, at least isolate it from all others until the occurrence of the miracle you await. Who knows? It just may happen.

Pest and Disease Control

Methods for ridding plants of pests and diseases fall into three general categories: mechanical, organic, and chemical. Mechanical controls are an environmentalist's delight and always provide the preferred line of first attack against problems. These controls involve physically removing insects or mites and diseased plant parts, usually leaves. Mechanical controls are safe, clean, and generally effective.

More adventurous gardeners spray homemade organic concoctions on pest-ridden plants. These, too, are environmentally sound. Often they are made from such common ingredients as fresh onions, garlic, peppers, scallions, strong-smelling herbs, and other malodorous plant parts. Combinations of these ingredients are crushed together in a food blender, strained through a fine sieve or cheesecloth, diluted with water, placed in an atomizer, and sprayed on the problem plants. I have not used many of these mixtures; I prefer mechanical controls for their ease—not to mention that many of these homemade cures smell absolutely vile. They do work, though, and since most organic pesticides have been developed by trial and error, feel free to let your scientific imagination go.

Chemical controls—insecticides, miticides, and fungicides—are effective when used properly. Unfortunately, most people either use them in outlandish doses, thereby polluting their homes, or use them at the first sign of a problem—before trying mechanical or organic control measures. I admit to the occasional use of pesticides and fungicides, but only after all else has failed.

Before you whip out chemicals be sure the problem is not a cultural one, and that the chemical you have selected is meant to control the *specific* pest or disease present. Insecticides will not control mites; miticides may not be harmful to insects; fungicides only work on fungi. READ THE LABEL. It should list the specific malady you seek to control and be recommended for use on plants grown *inside* the home. You must apply the correct product, in the proper dosage, and with a great deal of care. These products are toxic, and following the directions on the package is mandatory.

PESTS

The following pests are most frequently found on indoor plants. Effective mechanical controls are given beneath each pest description. For the most part, the mechanical controls are quite similar.

APHIDS: Also known as plant lice, aphids are usually 1/16 to 1/8 inch long when fully grown. They have oval or pear-shaped bodies with legs and antennae that seem long in relation to their size. They are usually green but may be yellow, white, gray, brown, black, or red. Aphids found on house plants are generally wingless, though there are also winged forms.

Aphids are quite prolific. They are usually found in colonies on rapidly growing shoots, on the undersides of leaves, and on developing buds. They cause a general loss of vigor, malformed flowers and foliage, yellowing, and wilting.

Aphids excrete a shiny, sticky substance commonly called "honeydew." The sweet honeydew attracts other pests, especially ants.

Control: I have successfully eradicated aphids by removing the adults with an alcohol-soaked cotton swab followed by a forceful spraying with tap water to remove the newborns and eggs. Do not forget to clean the undersides of leaves and along the stems where aphids are usually found. Severe infestation can be controlled by adding ½ teaspoon of household detergent to 1 gallon of water and giving the infested plant a sponge bath. Before this bath, cover the soil with aluminum foil to prevent the detergent from entering the container.

CYCLAMEN MITES: As their name implies, these pests have a special affinity for cyclamens. They are also common pests of African violets. Cyclamen mites are almost microscopic in size, about 1/50 of an inch long, and virtually transparent. They feed on leaves as well as developing shoots and buds. Infested plants become distorted in shape, and the leaves are more brittle than usual. Leaves and buds may turn purple or black, and flowers often become deformed or streaked. African violets become fuzzier than usual.

Control: Fact is stranger than fiction. Submerge infested plants (in their containers) into water which is 110° F. for about 15 minutes. Remove from the water and wave goodbye to the cyclamen mites, which are killed at this temperature. Unfortunately, the need for a laboratory thermometer is essential to this cure.

FUNGUS GNATS: Adult fungus gnats resemble common garden gnats. They are about 1/8 inch long, dark gray, and winged. The adults are not harmful, but their larvae, known as fungus maggots, can be very destructive. The maggots are wingless, beige, and also about 1/8 inch long. They live in potting soil where they feed on roots, causing stunting, yellowing, and foliage drop. Damage to the root system also leaves a plant more vulnerable to root rot.

Fungus gnats feed on decaying organic matter in the soil. Removing fallen leaves and other debris from soil surfaces will help prevent infestation. If you suspect the presence of this pest, check for maggots in the saucers beneath potted plants just after watering. The adults can be found flying around your plants after they have been watered or misted.

Control: Remove as much potting soil from around plant roots as possible and repot the plant in sterilized soil. Scrub saucers and containers thoroughly with hot water and detergent before re-using. Though mechanical controls are somewhat effective, the use of the insecticide malathion poured through the soil at a ratio of 1/2 teaspoon malathion to 1 quart of water is the only way to assure total eradication. Never pour this chemical through dry soil; make sure the potting medium is moistened throughout, or damage may occur.

MEALYBUGS: These critters are among the most common house plant pests. They have oval, flattened bodies, about 1/8 to 1/4 inch long, and are off-white in color. Mealybugs are covered with waxy threadlike structures which extend from the sides of their bodies and resemble legs. They are frequently detected by the presence of egg sacs, which look like loose swabs of cotton. The long-tailed mealybug, a frequently encountered variety, bears long "threads" at its posterior end. Mealybugs slowly crawl over plants, feeding as they go. They are most often found where leaves join the stem or at the base of developing buds. Mealybugs, like aphids, produce honeydew.

Infestation causes stunting and wilting and may cause early flower drop. Prolonged infestation results in the death of the plant.

Control: For the most part, mealybugs are controlled in the same manner as aphids. Picking them off with alcohol-soaked swabs and spraying the plant forcefully with tap water works beautifully.

SCALE INSECTS: Scale insects have a shell-like covering. The adults are usually 1/8 to 1/4 inch long. They are generally brown but may be gray or black. Some resemble hard black specks. Scales feed on the stems and leaves of a wide variety of house plants. They cause stunting, yellowing, leaf drop, and a decline in vigor. Scale insects also excrete honeydew—adding insult to the injury of their presence.

Scale insects appear in different stages of development. Young scales crawl about the plant, feeding as they go; adults locate themselves in a fixed position to feed. Scales are most effectively controlled during the crawling stage, when their outer covering is still soft and more easily penetrated by insecticides. Also, at this stage they are not as difficult to dislodge mechanically.

Control: Small populations of adult scale insects can be scraped off with a fingernail or a blunt knife. Cotton swabs dipped in alcohol are also effective. After picking off what you can, wash the infested plant with a forceful spraying of tap water to dislodge any stray crawlers. Otherwise, give the affected plant a sponge bath, using 1 gallon of water to which 1/2 teaspoon of household detergent has been added.

SPIDER MITES: These tiny pests seem to be the most common cause of complaint among indoor gardeners. They are red, green, black, or yellow; oval in shape; and have bristle-covered bodies. The most common form of spider mite has two spots on its back. However, this description may not help you since mites are difficult to detect with the naked eye. This invisibility often dumbfounds gardeners, who cannot figure out what is wrong with a plant that drops its leaves for no apparent reason. Other symptoms include yellowing and a lackluster appearance.

A suspect plant can be shaken over a blank piece of white paper where falling mites can be seen scampering for safety. They can be detected on the plant by the presence of fine silky webs on leaf undersides and at leaf axils, pin-sized holes on lower leaf surfaces, and ridges on the upper sides of the leaves.

Mites love the warm, dry atmosphere of our homes, especially during winter when the heat is on. The use of a pebble tray increases humidity and discourages infestation. Your plants will also love this treat.

Control: Forceful spraying with tap water greatly reduces the mite population. Infested plants should be washed at weekly intervals several times to remove newborns and unhatched eggs.

WHITEFLIES: As you might suspect from the name, these marauders, 1/16 to 1/8 of an inch long, look like tiny white flies. They feed on the undersides of leaves, causing foliage to pale, turn yellow, and then drop. Whiteflies excrete large quantities of honeydew.

Sometimes indoor gardeners do not realize this pest is present until the plant is accidently jostled, causing the whiteflies to take flight. Unfortunately, they will return to the original host and will probably infest nearby specimens as well.

Control: Forceful spraying with tap water usually controls whiteflies. The water should be as cold as possible, since these pests favor warmth.

DISEASES

Plant diseases caused by viruses, bacteria, and fungi can turn a lovely display into a nightmare. *Viruses* are microscopic organisms responsible for a number of plant diseases. They can spread to all plant parts and may be present without your knowledge until it is too late. Many viruses are spread by pests, particularly aphids, and by human hands. *Bacteria* are microscopic plants lacking chlorophyll and, like viruses, can enter a plant through wounds caused by rough handling or insect damage. *Fungi,* like bacteria, are minute plants lacking chlorophyll. They are responsible for most of the diseases affecting house plants.

Chemicals are effective against fungi, and there are dozens of fungicides on the market. However, the use and success of chemicals against viral or bacterial infections is uncommon. For the most part, these problems do not respond well to chemical treatment.

When it comes to plant disease, the cure often calls for tossing out an infected specimen to protect other members of a collection. It's frustrating. Many indoor gardeners foolishly attempt to wait a disease problem out, hoping a dramatic recovery will occur. However, infected plants do pose a serious threat to healthy specimens and should be isolated if kept.

The following diseases are those most often asked about by indoor gardeners. I have provided some tips on how to prevent each.

BACTERIAL LEAF SPOT: Darkened water-soaked areas on foliage, which may eventually fall out leaving a hole in the leaf, as well as light colored streaks on leaves and stems, often indicate bacterial leaf spot. While this problem is often misdiagnosed as fungus leaf spot, the more rapid spread of bacteria helps provide a clue to the real problem. The distinction may be purely academic, however, since both diseases are mechanically controlled the same way—by removing infected plants or plant parts as soon as damage appears. Since bacteria can enter plants through wounds, careful handling is one of the best protective measures. The use of sterilized potting soil is also helpful.

BLIGHT: The terrifying name of this disease, caused by fungi or bacteria, provides a clue to its seriousness. Tan or brown angular spots suddenly appear on foliage, stems, or flowers; a gray mold may cover infected areas; stems wither; and growth stops.

Excessive humidity and water splashed on the foliage encourage blight. A well-ventilated growing area and properly spaced plants help prevent this disease. A seriously blight-ridden plant should be destroyed. Specimens that are less severely damaged should be immediately isolated until the problem has been brought under control by removing affected plant parts or by spraying with a fungicide, which may help prevent spread.

CANKER: "Sores" or lesions appearing on stems or branches are called cankers. Cankers are usually elongated or rounded in shape, and they may be covered with corky, scab-like tissue. They are caused by fungi or bacteria and result in wilting despite an adequate moisture supply, yellowing of the foliage, and eventual leaf and flower bud drop. Gardenias are particularly prone to cankers.

Since the disease can enter through wounded tissue, care in handling is an important preventive measure. Small cankers found on the main stem, close to the soil line, may be gouged out with a clean sharp knife. Those appearing on smaller stems above soil level can simply be pruned off. Though neither control measure is guaranteed to save the plant, both are well worth trying.

DAMPING OFF: Damping off can affect seeds and seedlings of almost all plants, though some species are more susceptible than others. It causes seeds to rot before germinating (pre-emergence damping off) or just after they have sprouted (post-emergence damping off).

Prevention requires that seeds be planted in a sterilized, well-drained medium and that care be taken to meet the specific germinating requirements of each species. Infected seeds and seedlings should be discarded along with the soil in which they were planted.

FUNGUS LEAF SPOT: Fungus leaf spot is the disease most likely to affect house plants. Symptoms include spots of various sizes, shapes, and colors on leaf surfaces. A halo or a series of concentric circles around the spot is also common. A powdery growth may cover the spot, which then falls out leaving a "shot hole" in the leaf. Fungus leaf spot is encouraged by wet foliage and overly high humidity. Destroy infected plant parts as soon as damage is noticed.

MOSAIC: Mosaic viruses cause dark and light blotches on the leaves, creating a mosaic-like pattern. Plant growth may be stunted, discolored rings often appear on the foliage, and blossoms frequently fail to open properly. Orchids are particularly susceptible to this and other viruses.

Mosaic is spread easily from plant to plant by hands, tools, or pests. It is easy to figure out how to help prevent this malady. Keep things clean. Destroy infected plants and be sure not to propagate from diseased stock.

POWDERY MILDEW: The first signs of powdery mildew are round, white spots on leaf undersides. Eventually, both leaf surfaces become covered with a powdery fungus growth. Infected leaves turn yellow, then brown. High humidity, low light, poor ventilation, and overcrowding encourage this malady. The fungal spores are easily spread by the hands and by potting tools. Destroy infected plants or plant parts as soon as symptoms appear.

ROT: Rot diseases are caused by bacteria and fungi. Symptoms vary and include wilting; withered foliage; yellow leaves; soft, mushy or foul-smelling plant tissue; and a cottony gray mold. Overwatering encourages rot. Emptying the drip plates beneath pots 15 minutes after watering reduces the likelihood of infection. Destroy affected plants or plant parts. Cacti are especially prone to rot and are unlikely to recover once stricken.

SOOTY MOLD: Sooty mold often grows over the honeydew excreted by plant pests. It appears as a dark brown or black chalky coating. Damage is usually minor, and the fungus growth can be rubbed off with a damp cloth. Early control of insects will prevent sooty mold. Badly infected plant parts should be removed and destroyed.

WILT: Wilt diseases are caused by fungi or bacteria which clog the plant's vascular system, cutting off the water and nutrient supply. This malady is frequently mistaken for a lack of water. If correcting your watering practices and rechecking the plant's other cultural requirements do not improve its health, wilt should be suspected. Since wilt-causing organisms usually live in the soil, the use of a sterilized potting medium is the best protection against infection. Sometimes only part of the plant is affected. If that is the case, remove and destroy the diseased portion promptly.

GLOSSARY

The terms in this glossary are defined according to their use in this book.

Aereoles: That portion of a cactus from which leaves, spine, flowers, and wool are produced.

Bright indirect light: Light from an unobstructed window facing north; from a window facing east, west, or south, as long as translucent curtains are kept closed or Venetian blinds are drawn during the sunniest part of the day; or from a window facing east, west, or south, where strong light is obstructed by trees or a building. Bright light that is deflected or diluted in some way.

Chelate: (Pronounced keylate.) When chelates are applied to the soil, unlike simple iron compounds the iron does not combine with other elements to form insoluble compounds, but remains free to be readily used by the plants.

Cold frame: A box-like structure, placed outside, with a glass top sloped toward the sun, in which young plants and seedlings requiring protection can be grown.

Corm: An underground plant stem, or root, similar to a bulb.

Crown: That part of the stem at the surface of the soil, or the top of the plant, depending on context.

Epiphyte: Plants that grow on other plants, usually referred to as hosts, but that, unlike parasites, derive no sustenance from the host. Epiphytes are nourished by organic debris which collects and decomposes around their root systems.

Fish emulsion: A fertilizer based on processed fish parts.

Florets: Individual flowers that make up a larger flower cluster.

Genera: Plural of the word genus. A group of plants with certain similar characteristics. Every plant has a genus and a species.

Grooming: The removal of spent leaves and flowers; cleaning.

Habit: The general shape and form of plant growth, e.g., viney, upright, prostrate, weeping, bushy.

Hybrid: A plant resulting from a cross between parents that are genetically unlike.

Leaflet: One part of a compound leaf; a secondary leaf.

Medium: The soil mix or particular substance in which seeds are germinated.

Mulch: A protective covering applied to the soil surface around plants in order to reduce water loss, prevent weed growth, and prevent freezing. Commonly used mulches include shredded hardwood or leaves, pine needles, bark chips, and hay. Depending on the material used, mulches also serve to enhance the aesthetic appeal of a planting.

Offsets: Small bulbs formed at the base of larger mature bulbs, or small plants produced at the base of older plants or at the ends of shoots growing from the mother plant.

Perlite: A type of volcanic ash used to improve soil drainage and texture.

Plantlet: A little plant, usually found at the base of a larger plant; a miniature (clone) of the mother plant.

Pruning: Cutting of healthy tissue to promote plant growth or alter plant shape.

Rhizome: An underground stem distinguished from a root by the presence of nodes, buds, or scale-like leaves. Many plants, including some begonias, grow from rhizomes.

Sepals: The leaf-like structures that initially enclose the flower buds and eventually underlie them. The parts of a calyx, usually green.

Spadix: A fleshy flower spike surrounded by a leaf-like structure called a spathe. The spathe and spadix are found on members of the aroid family.

Sucker: A shoot arising from the roots or from beneath the soil surface.

Tuber: A modified stem structure which develops below ground; the most common example is the potato.

Vegetatively propagate: To propagate plants asexually, through leaf cuttings, stem cuttings, division, or air layering, rather than sexually— by planting seeds.

Vermiculite: A spongy, mica-like material used to improve soil texture. Also used for rooting plants.

MAIL ORDER SOURCES
OF PLANTS & SUPPLIES

GENERAL

Lauray of Salisbury
Rt. 41 (Undermountain Road)
Salisbury, CT 06068

Kartuz Greenhouses, Inc.
1408 Sunset Drive
Vista, CA 92083

Logee's Greenhouses
55 North Street
Danielson, CT 06239

Geo. W. Park Seed Co., Inc.
P.O. Box 31
Greenwood, SC 29647

AZALEAS

The Bovees Nursery
1737 S.W. Coronado
Portland, OR 97219

BULBS

Breck's
6523 N. Galena Road
Peoria, IL 61632

Van Bourgondien's
Box A-AH8
Rt. 109
Babylon, NY 11702

Royal Gardens
P.O. Box 588
Farmingdale, NJ 07727

Wayside Gardens
Hodges, SC 29695

White Flower Farm
Litchfield, CT 06759

BEGONIAS

The Thompson's
P.O. Drawer PP
Southampton, NY 11968

**GESNERIADS (African violets,
gloxinias, and related plants)**

Fischer Greenhouses
Oak Avenue
Dept. AH
Linwood, NJ 08221

Buell's Greenhouses, Inc.
P.O. Box 21818
Eastford, CT 06242

Lyndon Lyon Greenhouses, Inc.
14 Mutchler Street
Dolgeville, NY 13329

Tinari Greenhouses
2325 Valley Road
Huntingdon Valley, PA 19006

ORCHIDS

Green Valley Orchids
Rt. 1
Box 233 S.
Folsom, LA 70437

Laurel Orchids
18205 S.W. 157th Avenue
Miami, FL 33187

Fennell's Orchid Jungle
26705 S.W. 157th Avenue
Homestead, FL 33031

SUCCULENTS (including cacti)

Cactus Gem Nursery
Dept. H
10092 Mann Drive
Cupertino, CA 95014

Grigsby Cactus Gardens
2354 Bella Vista Drive
Vista, CA 92082

Singer's Growing Things
17806 Plummer Street
Northridge, CA 91324

Ed Storms, Inc.
P.O. Box 775
Azle, TX 76020

SEEDS

J.L. Hudson Seedsman
P.O. Box 1058
Redwood City, CA 94064

Thompson and Morgan
P.O. Box 100
Farmingdale, NJ 07727

SUPPLIES

Walter F. Nicke
Box 667G
Hudson, NY 12534

Gardener's Eden
P.O. Box 7307
San Francisco, CA 94120

Geo. W. Park Seed Co., Inc.
P.O. Box 31
Greenwood, SC 29647

Mellingers
AMH
North Lima, OH 44452

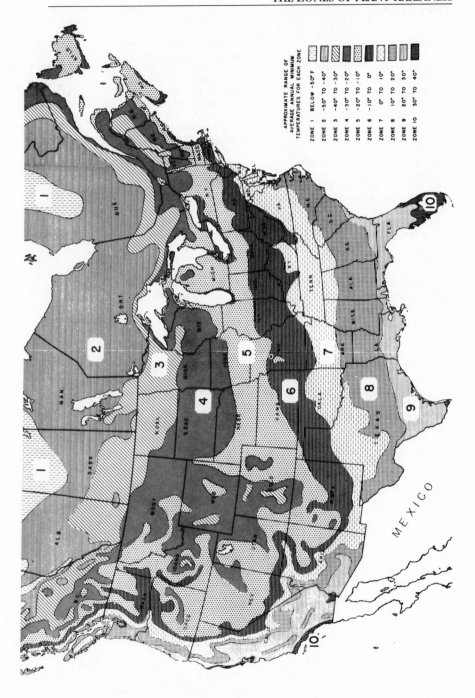

INDEX